M O D U L E

The Theory of Constraints and Throughput Accounting

Version 1.0

AUTHORS:

Monte Swain
Brigham Young University

Jan Bell
California State University Northridge

The authors are grateful to Karen Green for research assistance in preparing this module.

Contents
The Theory of Constraints and Throughput Accounting

ISBN 0-07-027589-0

Printed in the United States of America
    4 5 6 7 8 9 0   MZ   3 2

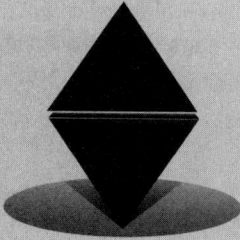

The Theory of Constraints and Throughput Accounting

GO TAKE A HIKE!

Imagine leading a group of 15 twelve-year-old boys on a 10-mile hike through the woods. As leader, you have two critical goals. First, you need to arrive at your destination, Devil's Gulch, in five hours. Ten miles in five hours simply requires that the group maintain an average pace of 2 miles per hour. Second, you need to arrive safely with *all* 15 boys—losing even one boy is obviously unacceptable!

As you survey your group, you're struck by the fact that there is tremendous variety within a group of twelve-year-old boys; the difference in height, weight, and physique is extraordinary. Clearly, some boys are better suited than others to hike 10 miles with a heavy backpack. With map in hand, you begin hiking, and the boys fall in behind you.

Because the trail is rather narrow, it's difficult to pass another hiker. Every time one boy stops to adjust his pack, to tie his shoe, or to throw a rock at a tree, others behind him are held up on the trail. This stopping and starting has little impact on boys near the front of the line, but the rippling effect causes increasingly more delays on boys further back. Yelling at individual boys to "hurry up!" doesn't appear to help much, since everyone needs to stop at least occasionally. By noon you are painfully aware that the group has only traveled roughly 3 miles. At this rate, you will arrive at your destination late.

During lunch, you call the boys together for a brief pep talk. The boys understand the need to pick up the pace and keep moving. With you in the lead, everyone attacks the trail after lunch with ferocity. Soon, though, you hear some arguing in the ranks behind you (what do you expect from 12-year-old boys?). When you turn around, you're a bit surprised to see that the group has separated itself into two groups. The group immediately behind you is spread out on the trail. The second group, much further back, is bunched behind a rather chubby young lad named Herbie.

Nobody wants to be stuck behind Herbie. So you decide to organize the group by speed with the fastest hiker in the front. Obviously, Herbie is the caboose, so you stay back with him.

Initially, this new arrangement appears to be succeeding. Everyone is able to go their maximum walking pace. However, soon the lead hiker is so far out in front that he is out of sight. Likely, he will make Devil's Gulch by 4:00 P.M. On the other hand, Herbie is really huffing under his heavy backpack. It appears that he won't make the destination until well after dark. As you reflect on your two goals from this morning, you realize that neither goal is being met. First, the group doesn't really "arrive" until *everyone* arrives, including Herbie. Worse, having the boys this spread out on the trail is definitely not a safe situation.

▲ STRATEGIC IMPLICATION OF CONSTRAINTS

A *constraint* is anything in an organization that limits it from moving toward or achieving its goal. The theory of constraints (TOC) is a way to manage constrained processes in order to maximize profits by increasing system throughput (defined as sales revenue less direct materials).

Managing a large business process is much like this hiking scenario. In a manufacturing or service organization, many processes depend on one another. Achieving a perfectly balanced production flow is nearly impossible. In the same manner that boys have their individual hiking speed, machines and people produce goods and services at different rates. Errors, maintenance needs, varying skill levels, and many other factors combine to create fluctuations among individual processes within an overall production operation. These fluctuations can create serious challenges to organizations trying to compete on quality, cost, and time.

▲ **Quality.** Individual processes often depend on one another. Work-in-process inventory is an output from one process waiting for another process. It is a natural result of fluctuations in processes (such as assembly, mounting, and insertion). Unmanaged constraints in a process inventory cause work-in-process inventory to pile up. Because work-in-process inventory can hide quality problems in both products and processes, it may take several days for workers to discover defects. Meanwhile, faulty output is produced.

▲ **Cost.** Traditional accounting methods often compute cost and efficiency variances for each individual process to help control costs in an organization. As a result, managers often produce units at or above budgeted capacity. This situation results in large inventories that tie up money and often create losses. TOC manages costs by discouraging inventory buildups and by increasing system throughput.

▲ **Time.** To compete effectively in the open market, companies must deliver products and services on time as promised. This task can be a major challenge when there are interdependencies among production processes. If each individual process is encouraged to produce at capacity, the overall organization can actually *slow down* because of the problems inherent with managing increasing levels of work-in-process inventory. Not only does a specific order have to work through each sequential process, it also has to work through the pile of work-in-process inventory in front of each process.

Key Point

When constraints in an operation are poorly managed, costs can go up, overall production time can slow down, and quality problems can go unchecked as unnecessary work-in-process inventory builds.

▲ PURPOSE OF THIS MODULE

Beginning in 1984 when Eliyahu M. Goldratt introduced TOC[1] in his book *The Goal*,[2] Goldratt and his boys-on-a-hike scenario have captured the imagination of many managers. TOC has had a strong effect on the way accountants provide information to business process managers.

The purpose of this module is to describe TOC and to demonstrate how TOC-based accounting, called throughput accounting, affects and is affected by traditional management accounting practices. We discuss the technical, behavioral, and cultural issues involved in merging throughput accounting with traditional accounting systems. After reading this module you should understand the following points:

▲ The relationship of the TOC model to an organization's strategy.

▲ The basic TOC model.

▲ The essentials of throughput accounting theory.

▲ The interfacing of throughput accounting with traditional accounting systems.

---

[1] Like many of the new management techniques, theory of constraints (TOC) has several synonyms such as synchronous manufacturing, optimized production technology; drum-buffer-rope systems; and constraint, bottleneck, or throughput management. The process of accounting for a TOC operating environment is called Throughput Accounting.

[2] E. M. Goldratt and J. Cox, *The Goal: A Process of Ongoing Improvement,* Croton-on-Hudson, NY, North River Press, 1984.

Exhibit 1
Strategic Position of TOC

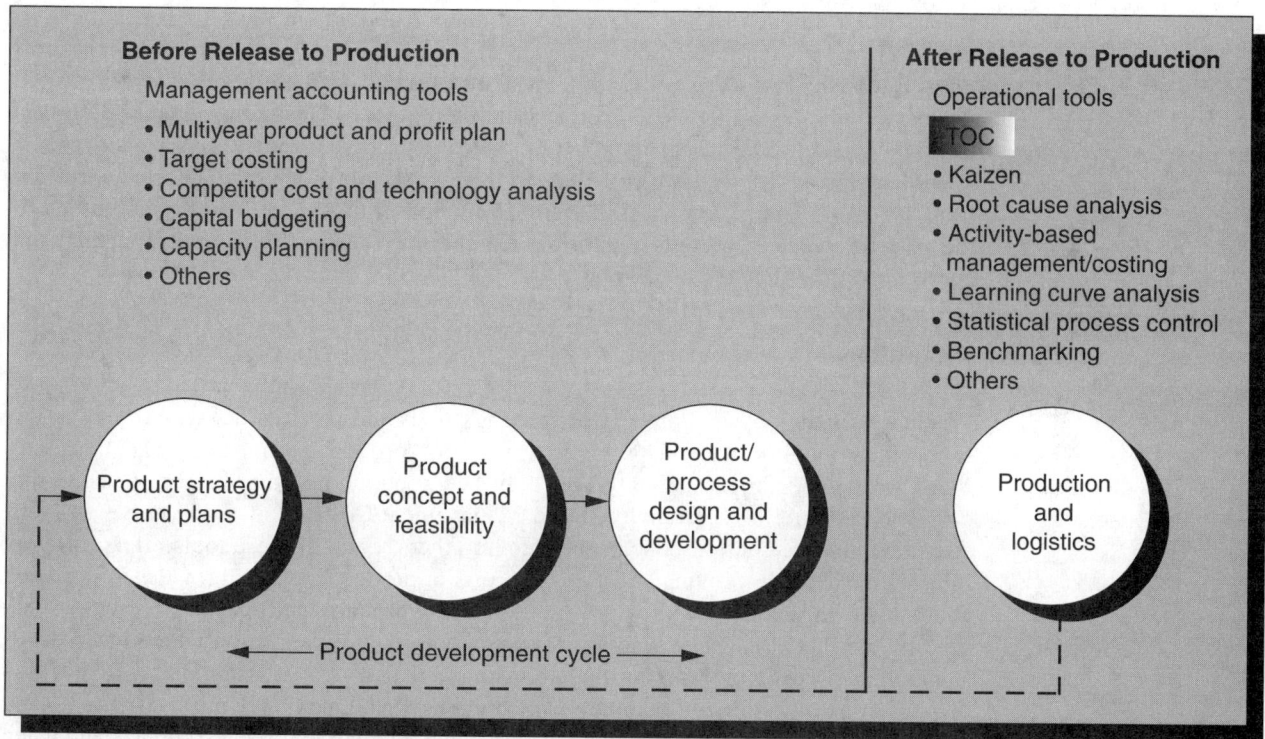

Before Release to Production

Management accounting tools

- Multiyear product and profit plan
- Target costing
- Competitor cost and technology analysis
- Capital budgeting
- Capacity planning
- Others

After Release to Production

Operational tools

- TOC
- Kaizen
- Root cause analysis
- Activity-based management/costing
- Learning curve analysis
- Statistical process control
- Benchmarking
- Others

Product strategy and plans → Product concept and feasibility → Product/process design and development → Production and logistics

◀—— Product development cycle ——▶

▲ The mechanics of throughput accounting.

▲ The technical, behavioral, and cultural attributes of throughput accounting.

▲ TOC LINKAGE TO PRODUCT STRATEGY

TOC is intimately linked to an organization's product strategy and its product development cycle. *Product strategy* defines the market segments the firm will sell in, the specific products to be produced for those markets, and the profits expected. TOC is one operational tool used to facilitate production of those products. TOC assures that daily activities produce the proper products and services to satisfy customer demand most profitably. It assures efficient use of existing capacity and identifies work processes that need immediate, additional resources to produce the products and services specified by product strategy.

Key Point

To get the most out of TOC, organizations must ensure that it is closely aligned with product strategy.

Product Development Cycle.

Exhibit 1 illustrates the activities that comprise the product development cycle and shows the strategic positioning of TOC. In discussing the development cycle, we use the term *product* to refer to physical goods, as well as services such as consulting, transportation, and entertainment. The product development cycle starts with high-level strategic planning. The result is a business, product, and profit plan that defines the market segments a firm intends to sell in and the products it intends to produce for this chosen niche. The next step in the product development cycle is to translate product and profit plans into specific product concepts. Product feasibility is determined by making preliminary estimates of life cycle cost, evaluating required investments in technology and training, and estimating capacity needs. Once a product concept is accepted and its feasibility tested, it goes into full-fledged design and development. Detailed specifications for manufacture and assembly are developed at this stage for physical goods. In the case of services, details regarding scheduling, responsibility and reporting, and communication lines are established.

Production.

Production is the physical process of creating goods and services. It involves day-to-day scheduling, monitoring, and problem solving for products, manpower, and machines. Many management tools support production: TOC, continuous improvement (kaizen), root cause analysis, ABM/C (Activity-Based Management/Costing), learning curve analysis, statistical process control, benchmarking, and others. Each of these tools offers different information about improving or estimating costs of production. TOC provides information about managing capacity optimally while producing products and delivering services specified by product strategy. It searches for areas within an organization where inventory is stockpiling or customers are waiting (a bottlenecked area) and determines how to redeploy manpower and machinery to eliminate the bottleneck and maximize profits. It shows how to use available capital equipment (capacity) and manpower to produce products and when to switch production from one product to another. It provides feedback for capacity planning about expenditures necessary to eliminate bottlenecks.

Key Point

> TOC is an operational tool that assists operating personnel to most efficiently produce the goods or provide the services specified in an organization's strategic plan.

▲ THE BASIC TOC MODEL

Solving the Hiking Dilemma.

Let us return to the hiking scenario. As the expedition leader, you face a dilemma. The boys are spreading out very fast on the trail, and Herbie is going slower and slower. You observe that Herbie loses ground for two reasons. First, he is simply slower than everyone else, on the trail. Second, every time the boy directly in front of Herbie stops to tie a shoe or look at a bird, Herbie must stop and wait. Each time this happens, you feel your irritation mounting. As frustrating as it is that Herbie is slow, it is even more exasperating to have him wait for someone who is actually a faster hiker.

Think Along

> How can you manage to keep the boys together and moving forward as fast as possible?

It is then that you realize Herbie is the key to achieving your two goals (safety and timeliness). Quickly, you call everyone together and have the boys line up exactly as they were on the trail. Then you have everyone hold hands, and you lead Herbie to the front of the line, effectively putting the group in reverse order! With the slowest boy (Herbie) now leading and the fastest boy bringing up the rear, you ensure that everyone stays together. Further, you reduce the effect of fluctuations in the overall hiking speed of the group. With the slowest boy in front, any time one of the other boys stops on the trail, it is relatively easy for everyone to catch up.

The remaining problem is that Herbie's speed now limits the entire group. Although everyone is safely bunched together, it is unlikely that the group will make Devil's Gulch before 6:00 P.M. You then realize that Herbie could go faster without a large, heavy backpack. You stop the group, explain your two goals, and propose to empty Herbie's backpack and share its contents among the hikers. Initially, the boys resist the idea until you explain that no one arrives at Devil's Gulch before Herbie. When the boys realize that they can carry more weight and still keep up with Herbie, everyone agrees.

Completing the analogy.

Hiking the trail is analogous to a production process. "Walked trail" is the product that the troop produces. The lead boy in the group starts the production process by beginning to walk. Then the second hiker processes the trail, followed by the boy behind him, and so on. Only after all 15 boys have walked the trail is the product fully processed. The rate at which this manufacturing plant (i.e., the troop of boys) produces product (i.e., walked trail) is solely a function of the slowest hiker's speed. Efforts to help other hikers speed up are wasted.

The amount of unwalked trail between each boy is analogous to work-in-process inventory. As boys spread out on the trail, work-in-process inventory is increasing. Hiking expenses increase as boys spend extra energy turning this work-in-process inventory into processed trail. Time spent hiking wrong trails, having to hurry to catch up with the next boy, or arguing about delays causes hiking (operational) expenses to increase unnecessarily.

To connect this analogy to actual business processes, consider the example of a computer manufacturer. Workers assemble the CPU (central processing unit) case, insert the motherboard, insert various driver cards (sound, monitor, input/output, etc.), mount the hard drive and floppy drive, and perform a quality check to ensure that the system functions properly. Obviously, no computer is complete until the last operation occurs.

Assume that quality inspection is the bottleneck operation. If production at preceding operations (case assembly, motherboard insertion, driver card insertions, and drive mounting) flow unchecked, a large amount of work-in-process inventory will build up in front of quality inspection. As these work-in-process inventories continue to build while waiting for the quality inspection to take place, inferior quality operations may be operating undetected. As a result, unnecessary costs accumulate.

Key Point
25

| Unnecessary work-in-process inventory can cause operational expenses to increase. |

Drums, buffers, and ropes.

Goldratt uses the idea of drums, buffers, and ropes to implement TOC in the typical operation where the bottlenecked operation is somewhere other than the beginning of the

Exhibit 2
Drums, Buffers, and Ropes in a Production Process

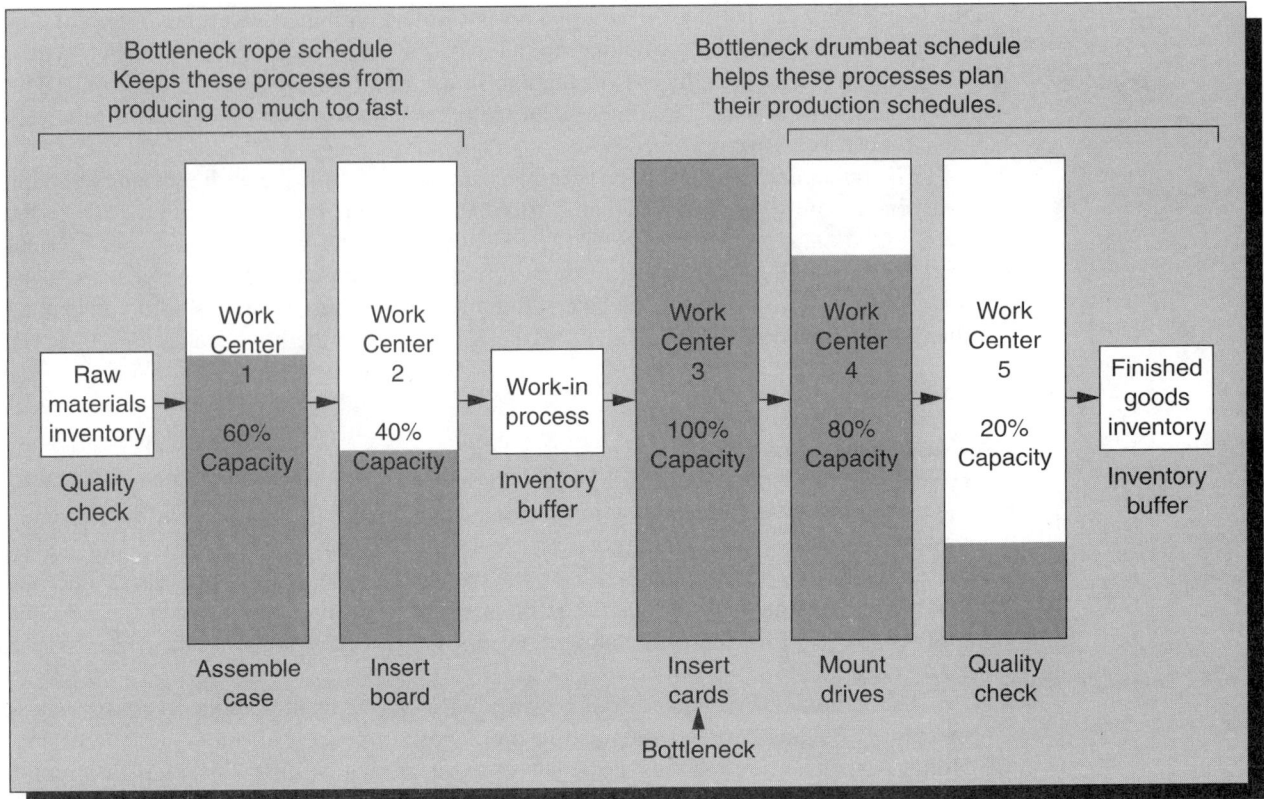

Bottleneck rope schedule
Keeps these proceses from
producing too much too fast.

Bottleneck drumbeat schedule
helps these processes plan
their production schedules.

| Raw materials inventory | Work Center 1 60% Capacity | Work Center 2 40% Capacity | Work-in process | Work Center 3 100% Capacity | Work Center 4 80% Capacity | Work Center 5 20% Capacity | Finished goods inventory |

Quality check

Assemble case

Insert board

Inventory buffer

Insert cards

Mount drives

Quality check

Inventory buffer

↑ Bottleneck

production process. A *drum* sets the tempo or pace of the work for the plant and is particularly useful for downstream operations (operations after the bottleneck) to help anticipate work-in-process inventory output flow from the bottleneck. Work-in-process inventory in front of the bottleneck forms the buffer and assures that the bottlenecked operation works at its maximum output and is not idle waiting for another upstream operation (operations before the bottleneck). The rope restrains the upstream operations from overloading the bottleneck with too much work-in-process inventory input flow.

For example, rather than quality control, suppose that inserting the various driver cards is the slowest operation in the computer assembly plant. The maximum number of computers the plant can assemble is limited to the maximum number of driver card insertions that can be made. The plant loses production time if the driver insertion operation has to wait for the motherboard insertion operation in front of it to finish its work. Nevertheless, you cannot simply move the driver card insertion operation to the front of the production line. CPU boxes have to be assembled and the motherboard card inserted before driver cards can be inserted.

Exhibit 2 graphically demonstrates how the drum-buffer-rope concept looks in the computer assembly plant.

In Exhibit 2, computers flow through the work centers from left to right. Exhibit 3 provides some production numbers for the computer assembly plant. Work Center 3 takes

20 minutes to insert all driver cards into a computer unit. Because this is more time per unit than any other work center, Work Center 3 is the bottleneck operation.

Think Along

Even though Work Center 5 (quality check) can actually inspect 120 computers each workday, it will not be able to inspect more than 24 computers because of the bottleneck operation in front of it. However, can Work Center 1 assemble more than 24 CPU cases per workday? More important, *should* Work Center 1 assemble more than 24 CPU cases per workday?

Exhibit 3
Production Data

Work Center	1	2	3	4	5
	Assemble	Insert	Insert	Mount	Check
Work description	Case	Board	Cards	Drives	Quality
Minutes per hour	60	60	60	60	60
Minutes per unit	÷12	÷8	÷20	÷16	÷4
Units per hour	5	7.5	3.0	3.75	15
Production hours per day	×8	×8	×8	×8	×8
Maximum units per day	40	60	24	30	120

Clearly, Work Center 3, as the bottleneck will limit the actual output of all downstream work centers (i.e., Work Centers 4 and 5) to 24 computers per day. However, upstream work centers (i.e., Work Centers 1 and 2) are not limited by the bottleneck (although Work Center 2 is limited to inserting motherboards in only 40 computers each day due to the production ceiling in Work Center 1). Nevertheless, these two work centers should *not* be allowed to assemble cases or insert motherboards faster than Work Center 3 can insert driver cards. If the production manager in this plant chooses to keep all centers working at their full potential, the result will be piles of work-in-process inventory. As noted earlier, high levels of inventory results in increased costs, decreased quality, and difficulty with timeliness. On the other hand, if the production manager (along with the management accountant) uses TOC to schedule the production process, the results will be as shown in Exhibit 4.

Exhibit 4
TOC Management of Work Processes

TOC-Based Schedule	1	2	3	4	5
	Assemble	Insert	Insert	Mount	Check
	Case	Board	Cards	Drives	Quality
Balanced units per day	24	24	24	24	24
Capacity used	60%	40%	100%	80%	20%
Work-in-progress inventory	0	3	0	0	0

In the TOC-based production schedule above, only Work Center 3 is working at full capacity. In addition, the only work-in-process inventory in the plant[3] is right in front of

---

[3] TOC is similar in many respects to the concept of just-in-time (JIT) management and production of inventory. Both concepts promote reducing work-in-process inventory in the plant to increase efficiency and eliminate waste. However, one fundamental difference between these two concepts is that TOC recognizes it is important to keep some work-in-process inventory in front of the bottleneck process to ensure that it is always operating at full capacity.

the bottleneck operation. The three work-in-process units in front of Work Center 3 serve as a buffer. The purpose of this inventory buffer is to ensure that Work Center 3 keeps operating in the event that either Work Center 2 or Work Center 1 slows or interrupts the production pace. With three work-in-process units at the bottleneck, either of the upstream work centers could shut down for as much as an hour (60 minutes ÷ 20 minutes per unit) without interrupting production at Work Center 3. If the two upstream operations worked perfectly well without any delays, breakdowns, scrapped products, or variety in how fast workers assemble cases and insert motherboards, then an inventory buffer in front of the bottleneck would be unnecessary. However, such perfection in the production of computers (and most other goods or services) is quite unrealistic.

The rope for the computer assembly plant is a production schedule that is based on the amount of time it takes the case assembly and motherboard insertion operations to prepare a computer unit to receive driver cards. The rope production schedule restrains these first two operations from producing work-in-process units faster than the bottleneck can insert driver cards. A similar production schedule serves as a drum to the drive mounting and quality inspection operations. The drum schedule allows these last two operations to anticipate exactly *when* they can expect the bottleneck to hand off computer units. As a result, these operations can complete final work on these units without unnecessary delay.

Key Point

Work-in-process inventory costs money and hides quality problems. However, having the bottleneck operation sit idle while other production operations that should have been faster scramble to catch up creates an irreplaceable loss of production output (i.e., throughput) in the overall process. Hence, work-in-process inventory in front of a constrained operation is necessary to avoid lost throughput.

Think Along

How might you decide how much of a work-in-process inventory buffer to maintain in front of a bottleneck?

Insufficient buffer inventory results in lost throughput and reduced profits. On the other hand, too much work-in-process inventory is an unnecessary expense and delays discovery of quality problems. Managers in TOC-based operations must make important trade-off decisions to determine the appropriate amount of inventory to keep in front of the bottleneck operation.

▲ DEVELOPING A TOC OPERATION

The goal of profit-seeking organizations is to maximize profit. It is important, though, that you understand that TOC defines profit in terms of throughput. *Throughput*, defined as the rate at which the system generates money, is calculated as revenue minus totally variable costs. The term *totally variable costs* usually means direct materials (and can also include other variable expenses, such as commissions, delivery costs, and other out-of-pocket selling costs). TOC is emphatic, however, that direct labor is not variable. However, field research shows that actual companies using TOC differ in their individual working definitions of totally variable costs. In at least one instance, a company used its current policy of radical downsizing to include direct labor as a variable cost.[4]

Key Point

> Throughput is used in TOC as both a measure of, and a management tool for, profit. Generally, throughput is measured as sales revenue minus the cost of direct materials expenditures (and out-of-pocket selling expenses, if any).

An organization managed using TOC will do three things to maximize throughput:

1. Establish sales prices higher than the totally variable costs (and out-of-pocket selling costs, if any).

2. Focus on providing goods or services that have the largest difference between totally variable cost and price.

3. Minimize the time between spending money to produce, and receiving money from selling, goods and services.

Sounds simple, right? Actually, all three of these things can be a challenge to accomplish consistently in a large organization. The key to effectively accomplishing these goals revolves around *constraint management*.

The Five-Step TOC Process.

Managing constraints in TOC is a five-step process:

Step 1: Identify the system's constraint(s).

Step 2: Decide how to exploit the system's constraint(s).

Step 3: Subordinate everything else to the preceding decision.

Step 4: Elevate the constraint(s).

Step 5: If a constraint has been broken, go back to step 1.

---

[4] E. Noreen, D. Smith, and J. T. Mackey. *The Theory of Constraints and Its Implications for Management Accounting,* Great Barrington, MA, North River Press. Research sponsored primarily by the IMA Foundation for Applied Research, Inc., and Price Waterhouse, LLP.

Exhibit 5
Bank Loan Process

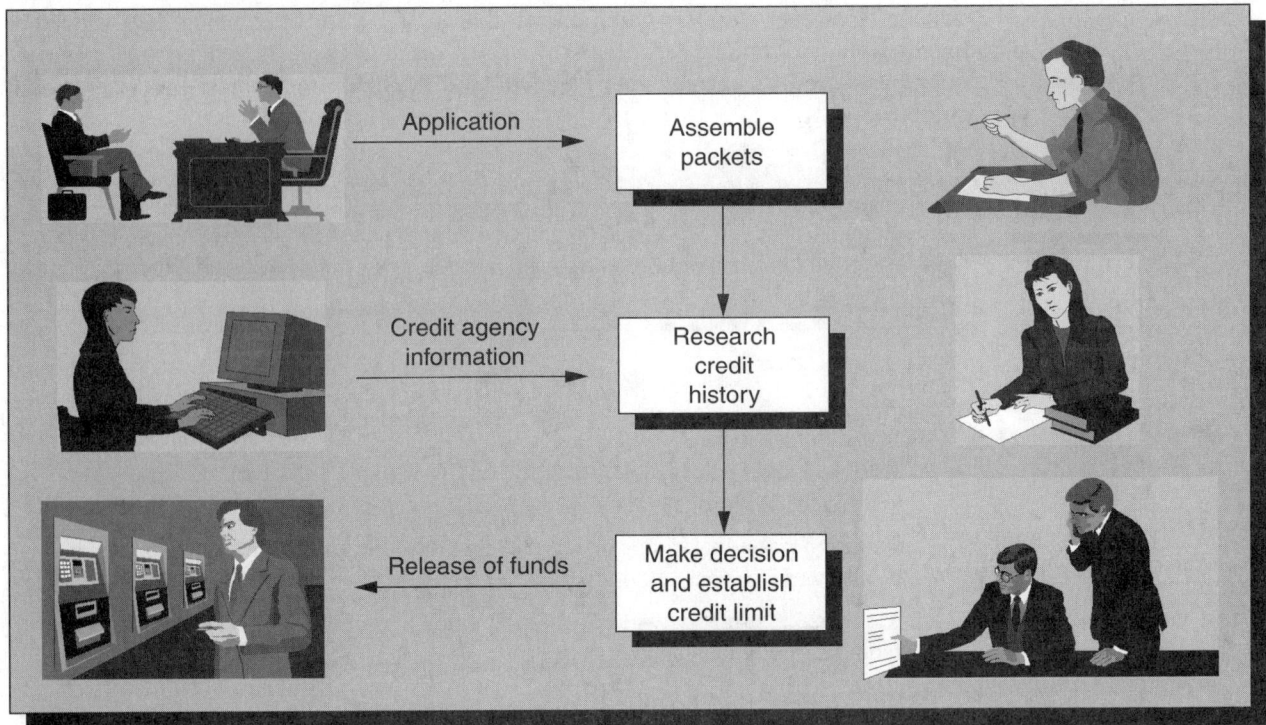

To help you understand these five steps, consider a loan department in a bank. Exhibit 5 illustrates the steps in the loan approval process. The process starts when the customer meets with an agent to initiate the loan application process. Once the customer has completed the application, a loan officer completes a three-step operation before the customer receives funds. The first step is to assemble the loan application with additional information from the customer's account. The second step requires working with credit agencies to establish a credit history on the applicant. The final step is to decide whether to extend a loan and to establish an appropriate credit limit.

Step 1: Identify the system's constraint(s).
Constraints can be classified as either internal constraints (internal to the organization) or external constraints (outside the organization).[5]

---

[5] See B. Atwater and M. L. Gagne, "The Theory of Constraints versus Contribution Margin Analysis for Product Mix Decisions," *Journal of Cost Management* (January/February 1997): 6–15. Also S. E. Fawcett and J. N. Pearson, "Understanding and Applying Constraint Management in Today's Manufacturing Environment," *Production and Inventory Management Journal* (Third Quarter 1991): 46–55.

Internal constraints include both process and policy constraints. *Process constraints* occur when a given process or operation in the company has insufficient capacity to fully satisfy market demand. *Policy constraints* occur when management or employee unions enforce a rule that limits an organization's operation abilities or restricts its flexibility (e.g., a freeze on overtime or hiring or a restriction on purchasing direct materials).

In the bank example, internal constraints may cause the loan department to struggle to get loans approved in a timely manner. The bottleneck is a process constraint if the loan officers are physically unable to perform the three steps on all loans requested in the time allotted. On the other hand, this internal constraint may be the result of a policy constraint. For example, if the bank requires every loan, regardless of loan size or the nature of the customer, to go through a formal approval process, a bottleneck may occur.

External constraints include material constraints and market constraints. *Material constraints* occur when an outside source of material becomes restricted. This can happen in the absence of adequate suppliers to meet the organization's needs or when regulations restrict a direct material source. *Market constraints* occur when market demand does not fully utilize a company's capacity to make the product. In other words, the company cannot sell all the products it can make.

Assume the bank is able to process all loans requested. A material constraint exists if the bank lacks sufficient loan funds to satisfy the number of loans that are approved. On the other hand, a market constraint exists if bank customers are not demanding as many loans as the bank is able and willing to supply.

Step 2: Decide how to exploit the system's constraints.

Once a bottleneck is identified, the organization must effectively maximize the money-making capacity of the bottleneck. Essentially, we must view an hour of downtime at a bottleneck operation very differently than an hour of downtime at a non-bottleneck operation. We should calculate the throughput yield per unit of the constrained resource. Using this calculation helps us measure the effectiveness of managing (i.e., exploiting) the constraint. For example, if loan officers are unable to process all loan applications, the accountant could measure the loan revenue potential of *each hour spent* approving loans. Alternatively, if the bottleneck is an external constraint (e.g., a lack of funds or a lack of demand), accountants could calculate the revenue potential of *each dollar loaned*. This calculation helps management to decide how and why exploiting the bottleneck will maximize the throughput of the system.

Step 3: Subordinate everything else to the preceding decision.

Once we decide the constraint that is to be exploited, we must treat all other constraints as secondary. Constraint management recognizes that increasing the productivity of a non-bottleneck operation does not necessarily contribute to profits and can cause inefficiencies for the bottleneck (that directly affect profits) by allowing unexpected work-in-process inventory to arrive at the bottleneck work center. Essentially, the nature of Goldratt's drum-buffer-rope system is to support this step of the TOC process. The bottom-line goal is to coordinate production efforts at non-bottleneck operations to keep the constraint operating at optimal capacity.

Step 4: Elevate the constraint(s).

TOC teaches that the best way *to make money in an operation is to elevate (improve) the capacity of the constraint* or bottleneck. Elevating the constraint can involve off-loading some of the processing work to non-bottleneck operations despite their less efficient production capability. For example, one way of elevating the process constraint in the loan approval process would be to assign much of the packet-assembly and credit-check work to less experienced bank clerks. Likely, the clerks will not be able to assemble packets and research credit histories as quickly as loan officers. However, the point of TOC is only to maximize the efficiency of the constraint operation in the loan process (the loan officers' time), not to maximize the efficiency of every operation in the overall process. (This approach can play havoc with traditional measures of efficiency based on traditional standard cost accounting systems.)

Typical methods of elevating constraints in other production examples include

▲ Adding more shifts.

▲ Scheduling overtime.

▲ Acquiring more equipment.

▲ Outsourcing some bottleneck work.

▲ Inspecting work-in-process inventory before it enters the bottleneck to ensure that bottleneck time is not wasted processing bad parts.

▲ Scheduling long production runs for the bottleneck operation to reduce the number of setups.

Note that applying these methods in *non-bottlenecked* operations is often a waste of process resources.

Step 5: If a constraint has been broken, go back to step 1.

As the organization works on elevating its constraints, other bottlenecks should emerge. These may be internal or external to the organization. The critical point here is that *there is always a constraint.*

Consider the bank loan example one more time. Elevating the capacity of the approval operation by using bank clerks to assist the loan officers will eventually lead to another constraint. Suppose the new constraint turns out to be a policy constraint—bank management will not extend consumer loans to clients who do not use the bank's VISA™ card services. Reconsideration of this policy leads to an exemption for customers who have checking accounts at the bank. Now the constraint shifts to outside the bank. There are not enough funds to supply all the demands for new loans (a "direct materials" constraint). Assume that the bank negotiates for more funds from an additional wholesale lending institution. Now the bank has the ability to process and provide more loans than clients are currently demanding; a market constraint has developed. With some effort, the bank marketing team is able to break this constraint by creating a special loan product tailored to the local college student community. Now the constraint shifts back inside the bank to the loan officers and bank clerks who are unable to process applications fast enough to keep up with demand.

Exhibit 6 illustrates the process of breaking constraints to discover new constraints.

Exhibit 6
The Cycle of Breaking Constraints in the Bank Loan Process

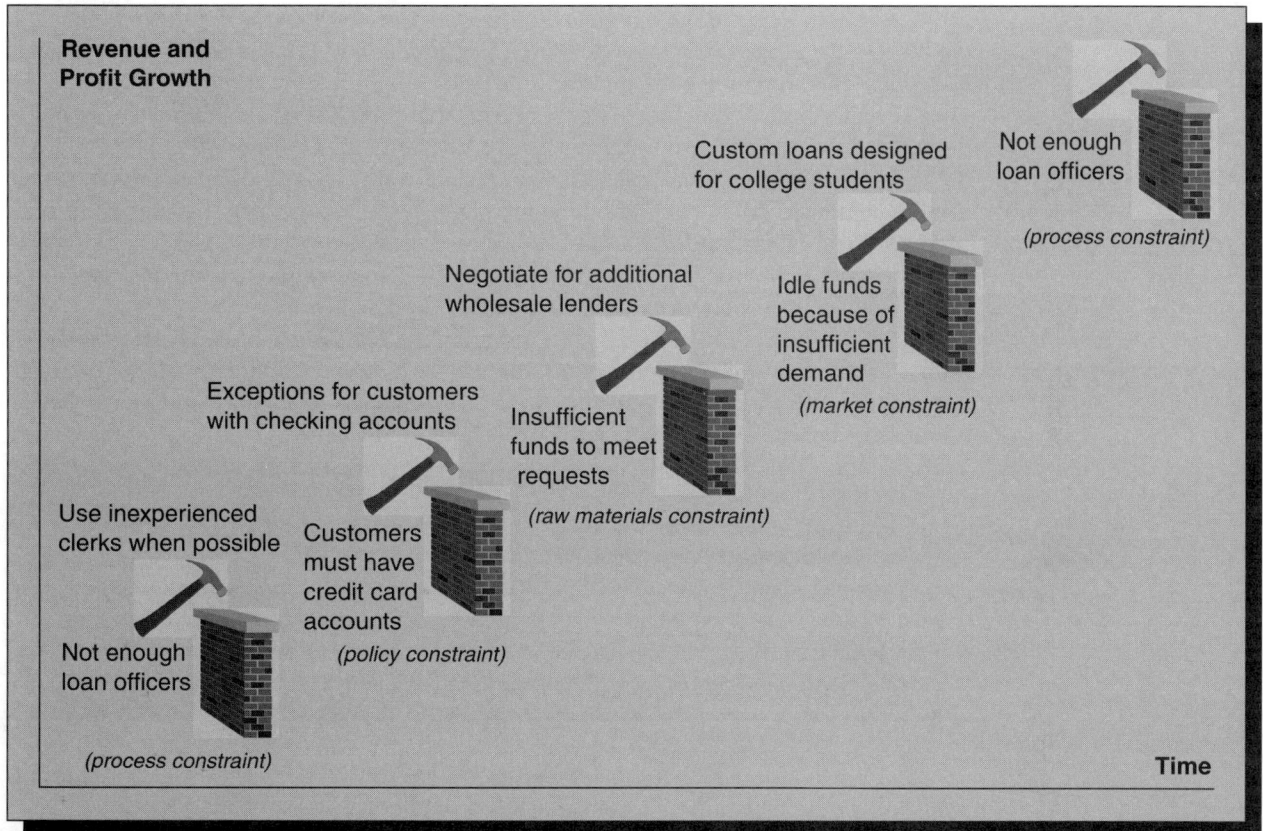

Revenue and
Profit Growth

Custom loans designed
for college students

Not enough
loan officers

(process constraint)

Negotiate for additional
wholesale lenders

Idle funds
because of
insufficient
demand

(market constraint)

Exceptions for customers
with checking accounts

Insufficient
funds to meet
requests

(raw materials constraint)

Use inexperienced
clerks when possible

Customers
must have
credit card
accounts

(policy constraint)

Not enough
loan officers

(process constraint)

Time

Key Point

The process of elevating and breaking a constraint must be consistent with the organization's product strategy. If not, the organization can move into new markets or offer new products or services that are not part of its long-term strategic direction.

▲ A COMPARISON OF THROUGHPUT AND TRADITIONAL ACCOUNTING SYSTEMS

Since about 1988, the term *throughput accounting* has been used to identify the assemblage of accounting systems, reports, and performance measures used to support a TOC implementation. It is important to understand that throughput accounting does not replace traditional managerial accounting methods. Throughput accounting supports a very specific and *extremely short-term* managerial view of an operation—the incremental value from a more effective employment of a constrained resource. It is not a strategic tool for making decisions about what products to produce and which customers to target.

New Accounting Definitions.

When Goldratt introduced TOC in 1984, he redefined two accounting terms: *throughput* and *operational expense*.[6] While the definitions of these terms vary in practice, this module follows the strict TOC-based definition that *throughput is sales revenue minus direct materials*. TOC throughput is similar to the traditional measure of *contribution margin*: sales revenue minus variable costs. However, there are important differences between throughput margin and contribution margin. The throughput measure assumes that the only variable costs are direct materials (and perhaps some out-of-pocket selling costs such as sales commissions). The contribution margin measure, on the other hand, typically categorizes direct labor and some manufacturing overhead as variable costs. The difference results from the time frame relevant to TOC. TOC focuses on maximizing short-term results—typically as measured within a matter of weeks.

The contribution margin definition of variable costs assumes a 6- to 12-month time frame. Think about this difference for a minute. Over a two- to three-week period, management is very reluctant to vary the level of direct labor and manufacturing overhead activities in a plant. To reduce or increase direct labor to handle a sudden two-week change in production would require management to hire and fire workers with abandon.[7]

Key Point

> The difference between throughput in TOC and the traditional accounting measure is *time*. TOC generally assumes a time frame for maximizing profits as a matter of weeks. The traditional measure of contribution margin implicitly assumes a time frame over several months. Consequently, contribution margin measures assume that direct labor costs are variable, whereas throughput margin measures assume direct labor to be a fixed cost.

Operational expense is all the money an organization spends to turn direct materials into throughput. Operational expense includes traditional *conversion costs* (direct labor and manufacturing overhead), as well as selling and general administrative expenses. TOC considers operational expense to be a fixed cost.

Generally accepted accounting principles (GAAP) requires that conversion costs be allocated to work-in-process and finished goods inventories. On the other hand, *TOC treats all costs, even direct material costs, as period expenses*. Therefore, whatever costs are consumed during the production period are expensed regardless of whether the goods or services in production have been completed or sold.[8]

Key Point

> Operational expense in TOC is the sum of all expenditures on production and administration activities other than expenditures on direct materials. TOC treats all costs (operational and direct materials) as period expenses.

---

[6] E. M. Goldratt and J. Cox. *The Goal: A Process of Ongoing Improvement,* Croton-on-Hudson, NY, North River Press, 1984.

[7] As we shorten the time horizon (say, one day or one week) or consider different decisions (such as purchase volume guarantees given to key suppliers), even the cost of direct materials becomes fixed. Conversely, over extremely long periods, most costs can be avoided. The idea that variable and fixed costs are relative to time, cost object, and decisions is very significant and is discussed fully in another module in this series titled *The Kaleidoscopic Nature of Costs*.

[8] To immediately expense all product costs (materials, labor, and overhead) regardless of inventory status is a gross violation of GAAP and the matching principle. Remember, though, that TOC does not emphasize cost tracking for reporting purposes. *Throughput accounting does not replace the organization's conventional accounting system*. However, many companies often run multiple types of information systems to support various needs of the organization.

Don't underestimate the significance of these new definitions for throughput and operational expense. Accountants have established a long tradition of measuring performance of cost, efficiency, and output using standard costs. The result of these standard costs systems are well-known performance measures such as labor efficiency variance and volume variance. On the other hand, performance measures of costs, efficiency, and output in a TOC-managed organization can be significantly different from performance measures based on traditional accounting models of standard costing. Standard costing is often inappropriate as a tool for management of a production or service process based on TOC and should be supplemented, or even replaced.[9]

A New Profit and Loss (P&L) Statement.

With these definitions, throughput accounting provides a P&L statement that is significantly different from the GAAP-approved income statement and the traditional contribution margin statement used by managerial accountants for the last several decades. Exhibit 7 presents P&L statements for a company that is producing and selling 100 tons of finished goods.

Exhibit 7
Comparing Three Profit and Loss Statements

GAAP Basis		Contribution Margin Basis		Throughput Basis	
Revenue	$500,000[a]	Revenue	$500,000[a]	Revenue	$500,000[a]
Cost of goods sold	(120,000)	Variable costs[b]	(155,000)	Direct materials	(50,000)
Gross margin	$380,000	Contribution margin	$345,000	Throughput margin	$450,000
Selling and general administrative expense	(350,000)	Fixed costs[c]	(315,000)	Operating expense[d]	(420,000)
Operating income	$30,000	Operating income	$30,000	Operating income	$30,000

[a] Sales price is $5,000 per ton, 100 tons produced and sold.
[b] Direct materials ($50,000) + direct labor ($20,000) + variable manufacturing overhead ($15,000) + variable selling and general administrative expense ($70,000).
[c] Fixed manufacturing overhead ($35,000) + fixed selling and general administrative expense ($280,000).
[d] All costs in the organization other than direct materials.

GAAP Assumptions	Contribution Margin Assumptions	Throughput Assumptions
• All direct labor and direct material costs are specifically assigned to inventory. • All manufacturing overhead costs are allocated to inventory using a predetermined overhead application rate. • Inventory costs are not expensed to the income statement until the inventory is sold.	• Only variable product costs (direct labor, direct material, and variable manufacturing overhead) are specifically assigned to inventory. • Rather than allocating to inventory, fixed manufacturing overhead costs are immediately expensed to the income statement. • Variable product costs are not expensed to the income statement until the inventory is sold.	• No costs (including direct materials costs) are specifically assigned to inventory. • All product costs are immediately expensed to the income statement, regardless of when inventory is sold.

[9] For a discussion of the effects of TOC on standard costing, see the forthcoming module in this series titled *Standard and Kaizen Cost Systems.*

The first panel of Exhibit 7 includes GAAP-based statements, the second provides contribution margin statements, and the third provides throughput margin statements. Note that the revenues and operating incomes are the same across all three formats; all that has changed is the way costs are categorized. It would seem that the differences between these three formats of the P&L statement are not that significant. What's important, though, is how these three formats affect the priority placed on managing costs, inventory, and throughput.

Think Along

How might GAAP inventory costing encourage building inventory beyond the ability to sell?

GAAP uses "absorption costing" that requires organizations to assign values to work-in-process and finished goods inventory based on the direct material, direct labor, and overhead costs employed in the production process. Because unsold units are inventory, they carry their share of these costs. These costs, rather than being expensed on the income statement in the period incurred, go on the balance sheet as *assets*. GAAP, therefore, *rewards organizations that build inventory*, even if the inventory cannot be sold. Hence, when costs cannot be reduced, they can be hidden by *increasing inventory*.[10]

Contribution margin statements cause managers to focus on reducing variable costs or emphasizing sales of products with higher contribution margins. Emphasizing contribution margin will lead managers to focus on increasing sales without encouraging them to build unnecessary inventory.

Throughput P&L statements emphasize increasing throughput by maximizing the use of bottlenecked operations or removing constraints. Emphasizing throughput in the organization also encourages decreasing inventory and increasing the rate of production.

A simplistic emphasis on contribution margin or increasing throughput, however, can cause managers to become too short-run oriented. One result is that they may ignore fixed costs in making strategic decisions such as product pricing. Another consequence may be to enter new markets or products without good strategic analysis.

Because contribution margin and throughput margin per product use accounting-based numbers, they do not provide information necessary for identifying or managing constraints. Many resources, such as equipment depreciation, are based on traditional measures of "practical capacity." Managing constraints requires physical measure of capacity that communicate to operations personnel.[11]

Using the numbers from Exhibit 7, Exhibit 8 contrasts GAAP and throughput profits under three production scenarios: constant inventory, build inventory, and shrink inventory. In all three scenarios, the company is selling 100 tons of finished goods, so the revenue is always the same. However, notice how profit levels vary.

Production equals sales in the first scenario, so inventory levels are unchanged, and profit does not vary between the two P&L statements. However, watch what happens when inventory levels start shifting! In the second scenario, the company makes more inventory than it can sell. Most managers and stockholders would agree that accumulating unnecessary inventory is both expensive and unwise, yet notice the conflicting signals of the two

---

[10] D. Dugdale, "Accounting for Throughput," *Management Accounting* (UK) (April 1996): 24–29.

[11] For a detailed discussion of the difference between traditional (accounting based) and contemporary (physical) measures of capacity see the *Measuring and Managing Capacity* module in this series.

Exhibit 8
Inventory Effects of GAAP versus Throughput Accounting

	GAAP Basis			Throughput Basis		
	Scenario 1 Constant Inventory	Scenario 2 Build Inventory	Scenario 3 Shrink Inventory	Scenario 1 Constant Inventory	Scenario 2 Build Inventory	Scenario 3 Shrink Inventory
Sales	100 tons	100 tons	100 tons	100 tons	100 tons	100 tons
Production	100 tons	110 tons	90 tons	100 tons	110 tons	90 tons
Revenue	$500,000	$500,000	$500,000	$500,000	$500,000	$500,000
Expenses						
Materials	50,000[a]	50,000[a]	50,000[a]	50,000[b]	55,000[c]	45,000[d]
Conversion	70,000[e]	63,636[f]	77,778[g]	70,000[h]	70,000[h]	70,000[h]
Selling and general administrative expense	350,000	350,000	350,000	350,000	350,000	350,000
Operating income	$30,000	$36,364	$22,222	$30,000	$25,000	$35,000

(Adapted from K. Constantinides and J. K. Shank, "Matching Accounting to Strategy: One Mill's Experience," *Management Accounting* [September 1994]: 32–36).

Assumptions: Sales price is $5,000 per ton; materials costs are $500 per ton, conversion costs (labor and manufacturing overhead are $70,000 per period.

Calculations:
[a] 100 tons sold × $500 per ton.
[b] 100 tons produced × $500 per ton.
[c] 110 tons produced × $500 per ton.
[d] 90 tons produced × $500 per ton.

[e] 100 tons sold × ($70,000 ÷ 100 tons produced).
[f] 100 tons sold × ($70,000 ÷ 110 tons produced).
[g] 100 tons sold × ($70,000 ÷ 90 tons produced).
[h] Assumed fixed in the short run at $70,000 per period.

P&L statements. The GAAP-basis statement appears to "reward" the company for increasing inventory by showing higher profits. On the other hand, the throughput statement appropriately shows the negative impact of increasing inventory. Finally, the third scenario shows the company reducing unnecessary inventory levels. Notice that the throughput basis P&L statement sends a positive signal for reducing inventory levels.

Note Pad

Calculate what profits would be in each scenario if inventory shifted between 95 and 105 tons. Verify how the GAAP-based P&L statement appears to "punish" management for decreasing inventory by displaying reduced profits, whereas the positive effects of decreasing inventory are appropriately displayed on the throughput P&L statement.

The differences in Exhibit 8 occur because throughput accounting does not absorb any costs to inventory. *All costs* are expensed as period costs under throughput accounting, *including materials costs*. Note also that, consistent with assumptions of throughput accounting, material costs vary as production levels change, and conversion costs (labor and overhead) stay fixed in the current period despite changes in production levels. On the other hand, a GAAP-based P&L statement requires all production costs (materials, labor, and overhead) to be absorbed to inventory based on production and are expensed only as finished goods are sold.

Key Point

In contrast to GAAP requirements, throughput accounting does not allocate any costs to inventory. Remember, though, *GAAP-approved financial accounting is not a goal of throughput accounting.*

▲ THE MECHANICS OF THROUGHPUT ACCOUNTING— AN ILLUSTRATION[12]

The Operation.

Exhibit 9 shows an operation that manufactures two products, hockey sticks and baseball bats, for Weston Company. Hockey sticks sell for $55 and have an average market demand of 100 units per week. Baseball bats sell for $60 with an average weekly demand of 50 units. There are three machines in Weston's operation and a final assembly area. Exhibit 9 shows the direct materials requirements, routing, and average time at each production operation for each product.

Each of the four operations, (the three machines and final assembly) has 2,400 minutes of production capacity in an average workweek (60 minutes per hour × 8 hours per day × 5 days per week). Because of cost concerns, Weston has a company policy forbidding the use of overtime. You should note at this point that there are *potentially* two different types of bottlenecks in the company. First, there is a market constraint, since Weston can sell only 100 hockey sticks and 50 bats each week. In addition, Weston has instituted a policy constraint (no overtime allowed) that keeps machines from producing at their maximum capacity.

Identifying the constraint.

According to the five-step TOC model, the first step for Weston is to identify its bottleneck. You can see in Exhibit 9 that there are four operations in this operation (three machines and a final assembly). If the market constraints are creating a bottleneck in the operation, then we should be able to produce 100 hockey sticks and 50 baseball bats each week without using more than 2,400 minutes in any of the four operations. On the other hand, if Weston's policy constraint is the bottleneck, then Weston will be unable to produce all the sticks and bats that the market demands.

Exhibit 10 multiplies the time used by each product in each operation by the weekly demand for that product and then sums that number across both products for each operation. Based on the data in Exhibit 10, it looks like Machine 2 would require 2,750 minutes of weekly processing time to produce all the sticks and bats the market demands. Weston's company policy limiting the production process to 2,400 weekly minutes at each operation has created a bottleneck at the Machine 2 operation.

---

[12] This example is adapted from B. Atwater and M. L. Gagne, "The Theory of Constraints versus Contribution Margin Analysis for Product Mix Decisions," *Journal of Cost Management* (January/February, 1997): 6–15.

Exhibit 9
Routing and General Information for Weston Company

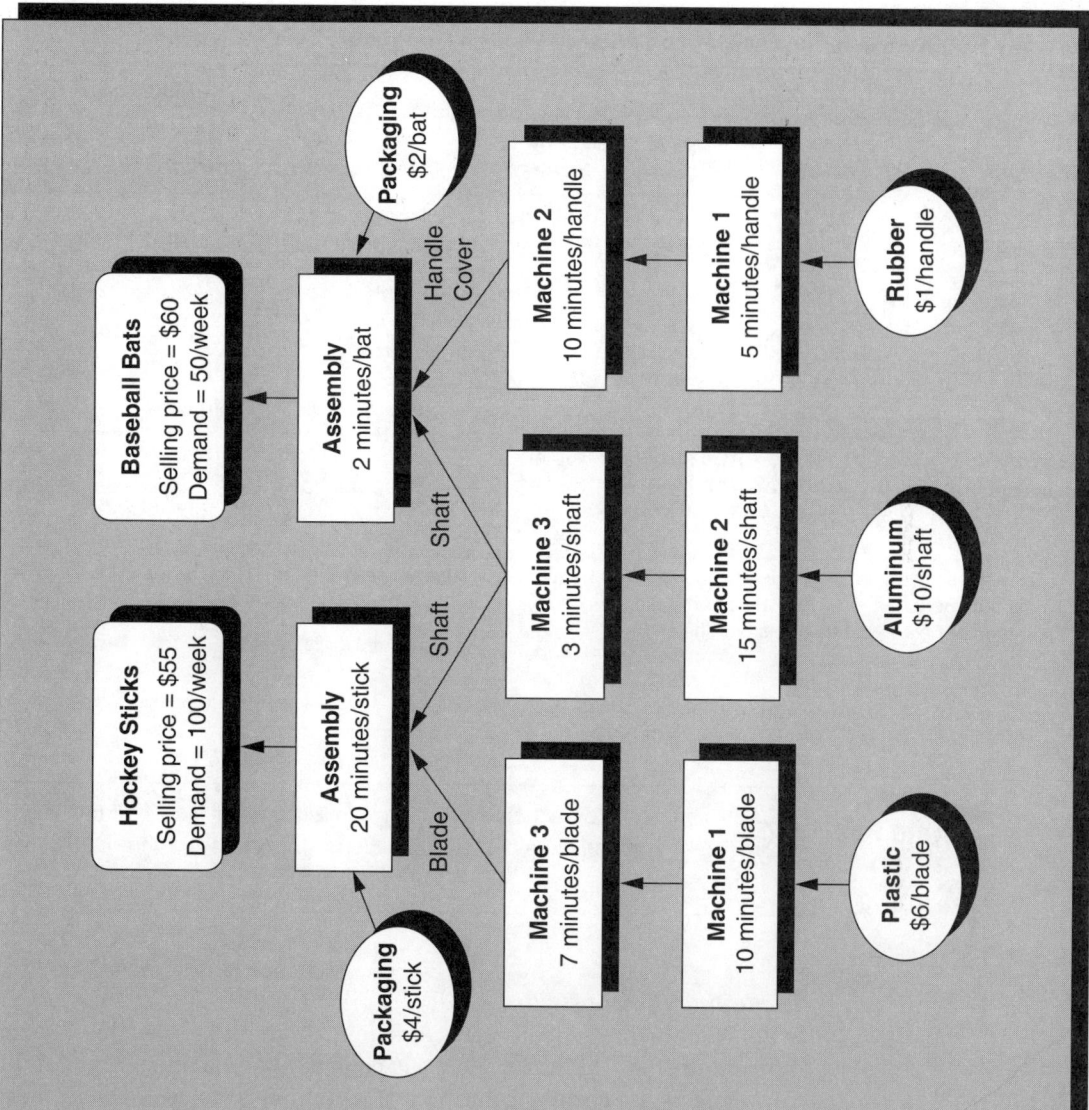

Packaging
$2/bat

Baseball Bats
Selling price = $60
Demand = 50/week

Assembly
2 minutes/bat

Handle Cover

Shaft

Machine 2
10 minutes/handle

Machine 1
5 minutes/handle

Rubber
$1/handle

Hockey Sticks
Selling price = $55
Demand = 100/week

Assembly
20 minutes/stick

Shaft

Shaft

Blade

Machine 3
3 minutes/shaft

Machine 2
15 minutes/shaft

Aluminum
$10/shaft

Machine 3
7 minutes/blade

Machine 1
10 minutes/blade

Plastic
$6/blade

Packaging
$4/stick

General Information

1. Weston employees work 40 hours/week and are currently operating with a freeze on overtime.

2. Weston currently has one one of each of the three machines.

3. Weston currently employs three machine operators and one assembler. The average direct labor pay is $6/hour for 160 total weekly hours.

4. Weston currently allocates manufacturing overhead on the basis of $9/direct labor hour (of this amount $7.20/hour is variable overhead).

5. The weekly operating expense for Weston is $3,000 (excluding raw material purchases). This amount includes $960 in direct labor ($6 × 160 hours), $1,440 in overhead ($9 × 160 hours), and $600 in selling and general administrative expenses.

Exhibit 10
Capacity Requirements for Each Work Center at Weston Company

	Machine 1				Machine 2		
Product	Time (minutes)	Weekly Demand	Capacity Needed	Product	Time (minutes)	Weekly Demand	Capacity Needed
Hockey stick	10	100 sticks	1,000	Hockey stick	15	100 sticks	1,500
Baseball bat	5	50 bats	250	Baseball bat	25[a]	50 bats	1,250
			1,250				2,750

	Machine 3				Assembly		
Product	Time (minutes)	Weekly Demand	Capacity Needed	Product	Time (minutes)	Weekly Demand	Capacity Needed
Hockey stick	10[b]	100 sticks	1,000	Hockey stick	20	100 sticks	2,000
Baseball bat	3	50 bats	150	Baseball bat	2	50 bats	100
			1,150				2,100

(Weekly capacity on each machine: 40 hours × 60 minutes = 2,400 minutes)
[a]15 minutes per shaft + 10 minutes per handle.
[b]7 minutes per blade + 3 minutes per shaft.

Note Pad

Calculate the numbers that would change in Exhibit 10 if it took 15 minutes (rather than 2 minutes) to assemble a baseball bat. Would this create a different bottleneck in Weston's operation?

Exploiting the constraint.

With the bottleneck identified as a policy constraint on Machine 2, management needs to determine how to best exploit this constraint to maximize profitability. Assume that Weston uses traditional contribution margin reports to manage this operation (see Exhibit 7 for an example of this report structure). Exhibit 11 summarizes all the data from Exhibit 9 necessary to compute both contribution margin and throughput per unit of finished goods.

Remember in TOC that the most important part of the overall process is the bottleneck operation. The product (a hockey stick or baseball bat) cannot be completed and delivered before the bottleneck has completed its operation. The basic approach to maximizing profits is to maximize the *profit per unit of constraint on the bottleneck operation.*

Exhibit 11 computes the contribution margin per minute of operation on the bottleneck operation for hockey sticks ($1.53 per minute) and baseball bats ($1.57 per minute). It also computes the throughput margin per minute of operation on the bottleneck operation for hockey sticks ($2.33 per minute) and baseball bats ($1.88 per minute).

These computations present conflicting strategies to Weston management. Based on the contribution margin calculation, baseball bats are top priority. Exhibit 12 shows that baseball

Exhibit 11
Summary of Product Information Based on Exhibit 10

Panel A	*Hockey Sticks*	*Baseball Bats*
Weekly demand	100 units	50 units
Selling price	$55.00/unit	$60.00/unit
Time		
Machine 1	10 minutes	5 minutes
Machine 2	15 minutes	25 minutes
Machine 3	10 minutes	3 minutes
Assembly	20 minutes	2 minutes
Total time	55 minutes	35 minutes
Raw materials		
Plastic	$ 6.00/stick	
Aluminum	$10.00/stick	$10.00/bat
Rubber		$ 1.00/bat
Packaging	$ 4.00/stick	$ 2.00/bat
Total materials	$20.00/stick	$13.00/bat
Direct labor @ $6.00/hour	$ 5.50/stick	$ 3.50/bat
Variable overhead @ $7.20/hour	$ 6.60/stick	$ 4.20/bat

Panel B **Contribution margin**		
(selling price−raw materials−direct labor− variable overhead)	$22.90/stick	$39.30/bat
Time on constraint (Machine 2)	÷15 minutes	÷25 minutes
Contribution margin per unit of constraint	$1.53/minute	$1.57/minute
Production priority	Priority 2	Priority 1

Panel C **Throughput value**		
(selling price − cost of raw materials)	$35.00/stick	$47.00/bat
Time on constraint (Machine 2)	÷15 minutes	÷25 minutes
Throughput margin per unit of constraint	$2.33/minute	$1.88/minute
Production priority	Priority 1	Priority 2

bats can be produced up to the 50 unit market demand. Producing the 50 baseball bats will require 1,250 minutes of processing time on Machine 2. After producing the 50 bats, Machine 2 has 1,150 minutes available to produce hockey sticks. At 15 minutes a hockey stick, Weston can produce 76 sticks (1,150 total minutes available ÷ 15 minutes per stick).

Exhibit 13 calculates that $2,010 in weekly profit would be created and reported using contribution margin analysis.

Think Along

What is the importance of emphasizing throughput per bottleneck minute rather than throughput per hockey stick or per baseball bat?

Exhibit 12
Optimal Product Mix for Weston Company

Column 1	Column 2	Column 3	Column 4	Column 5	Column 6	Column 7*
Priority	Product	Weekly Demand	Processing Time per Unit on Constraint (Machine 2)	Capacity Needed On Constraint (Machine 2) [3 × 4]	Capacity Available on Constraint (Machine 2)	Optimal Quantity Produced [(lesser of 5 or 6) ÷ 4]
Using Contribution Margin						
1	Baseball bats	50 bats	25 min.	1,250 min	2,400 min. −1,250 min.	50 bats
2	Hockey sticks	100 sticks	15 min.	1,500 min	1,150 min.	76 sticks
Using Throughput Margin						
1	Hockey sticks	100 sticks	15 min.	1,500 min	2,400 min. −1,500 min.	100 sticks
2	Baseball bats	50 bats	25 min.	1,250 min	900 min.	36 bats

*The number in column 7 represents the amount of each finished product produced each week. If the number calculated in column 7 is a fraction, it is truncated based on the assumption that partial units cannot be produced.

Throughput value calculations suggest a different product mix than contribution margin. Returning to Exhibit 11, the throughput value calculations per minute on Machine 2 suggest that Weston first produce all the hockey sticks that the market demands and then use remaining bottleneck capacity to produce baseball bats.

Exhibit 12 demonstrates that producing all 100 hockey sticks demanded each week by the market will leave 900 minutes (2,400 available minutes − [100 sticks × 15 minutes per stick]) available on Machine 2 to produce baseball bats. At 25 minutes per baseball bat, Weston can produce 36 bats (900 total minutes available ÷ 25 minutes per bat).

The new product mix of 100 sticks and 36 bats recommended by the throughput value analysis results in an increase of weekly profit to $2,192 as reported in Exhibit 13. As you can see, contribution margin analysis does not effectively manage the bottleneck to maximize the short-term profit potential of the Weston operation. Essentially, contribution margin analysis assumes that direct labor costs at the non-bottleneck operations can be avoided in the immediate future.

Key Point

Maximizing profit in a TOC-managed company is a function of maximizing the throughput return on the bottleneck operation.

Exhibit 13
Weekly Profit of Weston Company with Each Product Mix

Based on Contribution Margin

Revenues:		
(76 sticks × $55/stick)		$4,180
(50 bats × $60/bat)		3,000
Total revenue		$7,180
Less raw material costs:		
(76 sticks × $20/stick)	$1,520	
(50 bats × $13/bat)	650	(2,170)
Throughput value		$5,010
Less operating expenses:		(3,000)
Weekly profit		$2,010

Based on Throughput Margin

Revenues:		
(100 sticks × $55/stick)		$5,500
(36 bats × $60/bat)		2,160
Total revenue		$7,660
Less raw material costs:		
(100 sticks × $20/stick)	$2,000	
(36 bats × $13/bat)	468	(2,468)
Throughput value		$5,192
Less operating expenses:		(3,000)
Weekly profit		$2,192

Subordinating everything else to the constraint.

With Weston producing 100 hockey sticks and 36 baseball bats, it is obviously not satisfying market demand for baseball bats. However, the only way Weston can make more bats (without changing its overtime policy) is to reduce the number of hockey sticks produced. *Weston must subordinate market demand for baseball bats to the profit potential in producing hockey sticks.*

Note Pad

Play with these numbers for a minute. With an optimal product mix of 100 hockey sticks and 36 baseball bats, return to Exhibit 10 and calculate the minutes of excess capacity at each non-bottleneck operation.[13]

Think Along

Weston's management may be tempted by the unused capacity at Machines 1 and 3 and in the assembly work center. What should Weston do with all this excess capacity in its production process? If Weston chooses to use this capacity to produce more units at each non-bottleneck operation, what will happen? Will Weston be able to produce and sell more hockey sticks or baseball bats?

---

[13] Hint: excess capacity at Machine 1 = 2,400 minutes total capacity − (100 sticks × 10 processing minutes) − (36 bats × 5 processing minutes) = 1,220 minutes

Clearly, Weston cannot use the excess capacity in its non-bottleneck operations to produce more salable hockey sticks or baseball bats. The only thing that Weston can do is produce more work-in-process inventory. Now return to Exhibit 9 and try to envision where the inventory will start piling up if Weston runs Machines 1 and 3 and the assembly work center at full capacity. Plastic blades for hockey sticks will start piling up rapidly in front of the hockey stick assembly work area waiting for aluminum shafts. In addition, partly processed rubber handle covers for baseball bats will start piling up in front of Machine 2 faster than they can be machined.

Essentially, three things will result from this work-in-process inventory (and none of them will be good).

1. Weston will spend money purchasing plastic and rubber that it cannot turn into throughput.
2. As the pile of rubber handles start building, the Machine 2 operator could easily become confused. Rather than maching aluminum shafts, the Machine 2 operator might spend valuable time machining rubber handle covers. These covers will then simply create a pile of work-in-process in front of the assembly work center.
3. Piles of plastic hockey stick blades or rubber baseball bat handles could hide production flaws that remain undiscovered for some time. Once the flaws are discovered, Machine 2 may be forced to sit idle until acceptable rubber handles are produced. In addition, market demand for hockey sticks may go unfilled while Weston scrambles to produce hockey stick blades on machines that originally had plenty of time (capacity) to produce acceptable blades.

To avoid these problems, Weston needs to subordinate the non-bottleneck operations to Machine 2 using Goldratt's drum-buffer-rope system. Weston should first establish a buffer of aluminum (direct material) and work-in-process bat handle covers in front of Machine 2. This buffer should be just large enough to ensure that, in case Weston's supply of aluminum or Machine 1 runs into some temporary problems, Machine 2 can continue production.[14] Second, Weston needs to "throw a rope around" Machine 1 to keep it from producing more work-in-process blades than Machine 2 can support. Essentially, Machine 2 sets the production capacity for the entire operation. Finally, the output rate (drum beat) of Machine 2 is communicated to the assembly work center and to Machine 3 so that these operations can set their own production pace at a rate slower than their potential.

Think Along

> Look at Exhibit 9. Once TOC is implemented, where are the buffer inventories? Where is the rope? Which operations are affected by the "drum beat"?

Elevate the constraint.

With TOC and throughput accounting information reports, Weston management will naturally focus on elevating the Machine 2 bottleneck in order to produce more baseball bats (the market demand for hockey sticks is fully satisfied). For example, throughput value computations as displayed in Exhibit 11, panel C demonstrate that a 25-minute increase in processing time on Machine 2 adds $47.00 to weekly profit. Therefore, if the overtime premium is less than $112.80 per hour ([$47.00 ÷ 25 minutes] × 60 minutes), Weston should definitely reconsider its overtime policy.

---

[14] This buffer is very similar to what traditional managerial accounting would call a "safety stock."

In addition, Weston will also want to consider methods to increase market demand for hockey sticks. The throughput value data on Exhibit 11 shows that increasing weekly market demand from 100 to 105 hockey sticks adds $175.00 to weekly hockey stick profit (75 minutes to produce 5 sticks × $35.00). Note producing five additional sticks will cost $141 in weekly baseball bat profit (75 minutes to produce 3 bats × $47.00). However, the trade-off (if available) makes financial sense.

Think Along

> What other constraints might develop as Weston Company elevates the current bottleneck?

Eventually, as Weston elevates its current critical constraints (Machine 2 capacity and market demand for hockey sticks), the bottleneck will be broken and *will shift to a new constraint*. For example, Weston may find itself unable to obtain sufficient plastic to satisfy elevated process capacity and market demand. Now the whole TOC process starts again with new throughput value calculations based on units of direct materials (plastic) serving as the bottleneck resource.

▲ ATTRIBUTES OF THROUGHPUT ACCOUNTING

As TOC and throughput accounting continue to gain prominence as models of management, it is important to understand the technical, behavioral, and cultural attributes of this management system.

Technical Attributes.

By enhancing process understanding within the organization, TOC and throughput accounting provide information that is relevant to making good decisions.

Decision relevance.
Much of the management focus in a TOC operation is on the bottleneck. Because of its central importance to the organization's overall capability to make money, the bottleneck must necessarily receive the lion's share of management attention. Managerial accounting, if properly used, actually plays an important part in the management of bottlenecks by improving capacity use and by avoiding inventory buildup.

TOC improves capacity use decisions. Employees often identify bottlenecks by observing the buildup of work-in-process inventory beside workstations. The capacity of bottlenecked activities must not be wasted. Once employees identify bottlenecks, schedules and budgets for bottlenecked equipment and processes are developed and tightly controlled. Management accountants report and investigate unfavorable operating efficiency and volume variances immediately. If elevating a constraint means investing in additional capacity, then managers request additional capital budget expenditures.

TOC and throughput accounting avoid costly buildup of inventories. TOC focuses on maximizing throughput (sales revenue minus direct materials). It places no asset value on inventory but expenses it in the period in which the company incurs its cost. This approach discourages workers from producing for inventory. Because inventory creates holding costs, may become obsolete, and may contain quality defects, TOC reduces costs and risks for organizations.

TOC and throughput accounting are not the only accounting measures needed. Throughput accounting is not going to provide *all the information* management needs to make all decisions in an organization. Throughput accounting is *not* a cost system. It does not support the allocation of product costs (which an ABC system does). Management will have a very difficult time using a throughput accounting system to assess individual product costs based on investments in and use of materials, labor, and overhead. Further, throughput accounting will not integrate with the GAAP-based general ledger system. Hence, organizations will also need to invest in traditional costing or ABC systems.

Key Point

> Throughput accounting is useful for supporting effective constraint management.
> Managing product costs will require a separate product cost system such as ABC.

Process understanding.

TOC requires a thorough understanding of work processes: the flow of product from one operation to another, as well as the capacity and throughput time of each. Throughput accounting provides a financial, systemwide view of the organization. The efficiency or effectiveness of any single employee or production operation is important, only to the extent that the employee or operation supports efficient exploitation of a bottleneck to maximize throughput. Throughput accounting, in concert with the five-step TOC management model, allows the organization to design around a bottleneck to maximize the system's capability to make money. It recognizes that producing to capacity at individual operations within a process does not optimize the output from the process as a whole.

Behavioral Attributes.

Whenever information systems change and management introduces new performance measurements, behaviors are affected. Being aware of the behavioral effects a throughput accounting system can have within the organization will help enhance the benefits of the TOC management model, as well as minimize potential conflicts caused by changing the company's information structure.

Benefit: Avoids local optimization.

Throughput accounting encourages cooperation throughout the organization to achieve company profit goals, instead of rewarding employees for optimizing individual processes. TOC uses the capacity of a bottleneck to set standards for all operations. When negative capacity-use variances start appearing in the plant, management promptly determines their underlying causes. If the bottleneck happens to be performing below its capacity, then all other processes must scale back production. Management needs to get the bottleneck processes back up to standard volume levels as soon as possible.

Benefit: Improves communication between departments.

TOC communicates the needs and the capacity of the bottleneck. *The drumbeat* of the bottleneck is the production schedule that non-bottleneck, downstream operations use to schedule the parts and people needed to complete production and deliver products to customers. *The bottleneck rope* is the production schedule for upstream, non-bottleneck operations. It specifies a work schedule such that the bottleneck receives sufficient output from upstream operations without an unnecessary buildup of work-in-process inventory.

Work-in-process inventory is also a communication device in TOC. A dangerously low *buffer of inventory* in front of the bottleneck immediately signals upstream operations to use their excess capacity to expedite (i.e., hurry up) their production to ensure the bottleneck is not "starved" for parts.

Key Point

> The essence of TOC and throughput accounting is communication throughout the organization that helps everyone coordinate and focus on enhancing the profit-making potential of the company.

Potential conflict: Excessive budget cuts.

A poorly used throughput accounting system can create problems. For example, the excess capacity in Machines 1 and 3 and in the assembly work center may tempt management at Weston Company to make severe budget cuts within these non-bottleneck processes, particularly in times of economic stress. Understandably, employees in these non-bottleneck work centers may become concerned that their jobs could be in jeopardy. Before Weston releases workers and scales back production capacity, management needs to bear in mind that it is impossible in most operations to balance individual process capacities.

Like the boys in the opening hiking scenario, every operation within the process has inherently different capacities. Further, a company *needs* to identify a bottleneck to use as the focus for the rest of the organization. Herbie, our slow friend on the hiking trail, is not really a liability to the group's overall progress. By intelligently using him to establish pace, the wise hike leader is able to confidently project an arrival time and to minimize problems resulting from boys getting too spread out on the trail. Releasing non-bottleneck workers in order to reduce capacity can remove the flexibility necessary in the enterprise to implement a TOC system. Further, effective TOC requires cooperation throughout the organization. Employees at Weston Company are not likely to cooperate with the TOC system if they are afraid that creating large amounts of slack in their operations could cost them their jobs.

Potential conflict: Lack of focus on non-bottlenecks.

As you have likely noticed by now, TOC is rather fanatic in the focus it places on management of bottleneck processes. The theory is that only by elevating bottlenecks can the organization save money or improve throughput. Although TOC does address the need to improve existing non-bottlenecks (in terms of supporting the bottleneck operation), there may be a risk that employees will focus very little time on improvement of non-bottlenecks. With the use of other established management approaches (such as ABM, quality costing, or target costing), employees can improve product quality, strengthen process productivity and timeliness, and reduce cost throughout the organization.

Potential conflict: Short-run behavior strategy.

Throughput accounting takes a very narrow view of costs to optimize the system in the very short run. There is a real danger that, like contribution margin analysis, TOC can lead to decisions that can harm the organization in the long-run. Consider the bank loan example. In elevating the loan funds available (materials) constraint, the bank created a new borrowers available (market) constraint. To elevate this constraint, the bank decided to make loans to a new class of customers—college students. Entering a new customer or product market, however, is a strategic decision that should not be made on the basis of short-run constraint elevation. Before elevating this constraint, the bank needs to redefine its product strategy, otherwise, it will enter a market it may not want to be in.

Key Point

> The focus of improvement in non-bottleneck processes should be on enhancing quality and throughput, not on reducing capacity or entering new product or customer markets. Otherwise, employees may be hesitant to support a TOC program, or the firm may incrementally commit itself to a new product strategy.

Cultural Attributes.

In addition to right behaviors, introducing and sustaining TOC in an organization requires appealing to and creating a set of shared cultural values, beliefs, and mindsets within an organization.

Creating a receptive culture for TOC.

Introducing a new process in an existing organizational culture is always hard. People have their existing beliefs, values, and mindsets. A new process that does not appeal to shared organizational values is unlikely to take hold. Upper management needs to strongly endorse TOC and demonstrate its power to improve profits. Management should use training, speeches, and internal literature to demonstrate the dollar impact of TOC on a business unit or product line that is familiar. Documenting each additional management success with TOC for all to celebrate helps induce others to change. This approach is much easier in an organizational environment that values continuous improvement and does not fear change.

Mindset change.

Making the shift to a TOC-based operation often requires that management make significant mindset adjustments. Organizations, perhaps reflective of Western culture, tend to value individual and local performance. Traditionally, an effectively managed operation is viewed as one that gets maximum output from each individual worker and process. This mindset permeates both manufacturing and service industries. In TOC the focus is on producing what customers want instead of the maximum output that workers are capable of producing. This concept requires a mindset shift in viewing a well-managed operation. A well-managed TOC operation identifies the products that customers want and then manages the operation to satisfy customer needs with high-quality, on-time products—regardless of the effect on the efficiency of individual workers or processes.

Exhibit 14 outlines more specifically how TOC affects managers' assumptions. Traditionally, supervisors and managers become very concerned when workers are idle; hence the pressure to "keep working." As soon as workers process one pile of materials, they find more materials and restart. With the focus on keeping the workers busy building inventory, often no one asks when, why, or how anyone will buy the stockpiled goods and services. The subtler (and more important) question is, Are we building the correct *amount* of the *right* inventory to make the most money for the organization?"

Key Point

> Sometimes an organization can become focused on keeping the production process busy all the time rather than on producing the right inventory at the right time.

Exhibit 14
The Assumptions versus The Facts

Prior Assumption	Current Fact
Keeping people busy is the key to making money.	A focus on labor utilization hinders cash flow due to high high inventory and the emphasis on keeping people busy.
By keeping utilization high, employees help the company perform well financially.	High utilization of resources does not correlate to profitability.
High labor-utilization rates ensure high levels of customer satisfaction.	High utilization of resources does not necessarily correlate to high customer satisfaction.
If managers release workers to other areas of the operation, they may not get them back when they need them.	Managers will willingly release workers to go where the work is when the right performance measures are used.
Traditional accounting standards tell managers whether they are effective as a total enterprise.	Traditional standards are subjective, inaccurate, and require constant monitoring.
Maximizing the production output per setup and building inventory is key to making money.	Making only what customers order is the key to making money, and on-time delivery is the critical success factor.

(Adapted from D. Westra, M. L. Srikanth, and M. Kane, "Measuring Operational Performance in a Throughput World," *Management Accounting* [April 1996]: 41–47.)

Creating cross-functional cooperation.

TOC implementation requires cooperation across functions and processes in an organization. Information has to be shared on customers' wants and on the availability of capacity. Teamwork must be the norm. Everyone in the organization must have a process view of the company. Everyone must work on elevating the constraint. Nonconstrained operations must subordinate their needs to the needs of the constraint. This mindset, in effect, creates a community of the organization. Think about the boys hiking in the woods. With Herbie as the focus of the group effort, each boy will certainly become much more aware of the need to get *everyone* to Devil's Gulch. Hence, everyone is more responsive to ideas like unloading some of Herbie's backpack weight to other backpacks. Similarly, TOC and throughput accounting encourage and require team participation in organizations.

▲ LESSONS LEARNED

▲ TOC is a relatively new management tool that identifies and uses constraints to maximize the profit potential of a company.

▲ Intelligent management of constraints (sometimes called bottlenecks) involves the following five steps: (1) identify the system's constraint, (2) decide how to exploit the system's constraint, (3) subordinate everything else to the preceding decision, (4) elevate the constraint, and (5) if a constraint has been broken, go back to step 1.

▲ A drum-buffer-rope approach is used to subordinate all other operations to the bottleneck. The "drum beat" sets the production pace for the rest of the operation. Upstream operations are held in check by a "rope" schedule. A minimal "buffer" of inventory kept in front of the bottleneck keeps it running at full capacity.

▲ Throughput accounting is a system specifically designed to support TOC-based management. The system has its own definition of some key accounting terms and its own P&L statement format.

▲ Throughput accounting defines throughput value as sales revenue minus the cost of direct materials expenditures (and any out-of-pocket selling expenses). Operational expense refers to all expenditures other than direct materials.

▲ Maximizing operating profit means maximizing throughput value per unit of bottlenecked capacity.

▲ Unlike GAAP-based P&L statements, throughput accounting does not promote overproduction of inventory.

▲ Throughput accounting assumes a shorter time period than the contribution margin P&L statements in defining variable costs. The former typically assumes weeks; the latter assumes 6 to 12 months.

▲ Throughput accounting systems focus on the efficiency and capacity of the *entire* process, rather than on individual operations and work centers. Only bottleneck operations are managed to maximize individual efficiencies and output volumes. The performance of non-bottlenecks is measured by how well they smoothly interface with the bottleneck to keep it operating efficiently without unnecessary buildup of work-in-process inventory.

▲ Throughput accounting is a short-term operations management tool. Other management accounting tools, such as target costing, product costing and ABC, are needed to address long-range strategic concerns.

APPENDIX—TOC AND LINEAR PROGRAMMING

▲ WHAT IS LINEAR PROGRAMMING?

You may have studied linear programming (LP) in a previous mathematics or business operations class. LP is a fairly rigorous mathematical method of solving practical problems such as allocation of resources by means of linear functions where the variables involved are subject to constraints. LP has been around a long time—much longer than TOC. Both concepts involve maximizing a function subject to constraints. There is a strong relationship between LP and TOC. In fact, LP can be used to help with the first two steps of the TOC process (identify the system's constraint, and decide how to exploit the system's constraint).

Exhibit 15 shows a typical LP solution to the Weston Company problem established earlier in Exhibit 12. See if you can identify where the information originally provided in Exhibit 9 sets up the programming equations in Exhibit 15.

This module does not cover the mathematics involved in an LP solution. Many software programs are available to business professionals who choose to use LP as a first step to designing a TOC system. One popular program (used to compute the solution in Exhibit 15) is Microsoft Excel™. The specific steps required to create the LP solution follow.[15]

Set Up the Problem.

1. Open Excel™ and set up your spreadsheet to look just like the top box in Exhibit 15.
2. Leave cells B6 and B7 blank (remember that we're trying to determine how many hockey sticks and baseball bats to produce).
3. Build formulas for the following cells:

$$B10: = B2 * B6$$
$$B11: = B3 * B7$$
$$B12: = -B4 * B6$$
$$B13: = -B5 * B7$$
$$B14: = SUM(B10 : B13)$$
$$B16: = B14 + B15$$
$$G6: = (E6 * B6) + (F6 * B7)$$
$$G7: = (E7 * B6) + (F7 * B7)$$
$$G8: = (E8 * B6) + (F8 * B7)$$
$$G9: = (E9 * B6) + (F9 * B7)$$
$$G10: = SUM(G6 : G9)$$

4. Test your formula by putting 75 in cell B6 and 25 in cell B7. The B16 cell should equal $800, and cell G10 should equal $5,000.

Solve the Problem.

1. Open Solver from the tools menu.[16] A box will appear titled "Solver Parameters".
2. "Set Target Cell" represents the objective function. Make sure this space is highlighted and then click on cell B16 (Profit) to enter the objective function. This space should now contain $B$16.

---

[15] The Excel solution method is adapted from R. Verma, "My Operations Management Students Love Linear Programming," *Decision Line* (July 1997): 9–12.

[16] If you don't see Solver as an option under Tools menu, then this module was not installed during Excel setup. *You must add this component using the Excel setup routine.* Use your Microsoft Office CD-ROM or installation disks to rerun the installation procedure on your computer. Select the option to add or delete components.

3. Check the "Max" button in the "Equal To" area (since we are maximizing profit in this problem).

4. Click on "By Changing Cells" area. You need to input the location of the two decision variables (Sticks Produced and Bats Produced) here. Therefore, highlight cells B6 and B7. This area should now contain $B$6:$B$7.

5. Click on "Add" to begin adding constraints. A box will appear titled "Add Constraint". Remember that there are two types of constraints at Weston— production constraints and market constraints.

6. Add the first production constraint by clicking on the "Cell Reference" area. Next click on cell G6 (Total Minutes on Machine 1). The "Cell Reference" area should now contain $G$6. Make sure the middle column (the mathematical operator) is set on <=. Click on the "Constraint" area. Then click on cell H6 (Ceiling for Machine 1). The "Constraint" area should now contain =$H$6. Click OK.

7. Add the remaining production constraints for the last three operations using the approach just followed for Machine 1.

8. Add the two market constraints using the approach just followed for the production constraints. Set cell B6 <= cell E12. Set cell B7 <= cell E13.

9. In the "Solver Parameters" box, click on the "Options" button. Check the box "Assume Linear Model" and click OK.

10. Click on "Solve" and a box titled "Solver Results" will appear. Note that cells B6 and B7 have been changed by the program to contain the optimal number of hockey sticks and baseball bats.

11. Highlight "Answer" and "Sensitivity" in the "Reports" area of the "Solver Results" box and click "OK". These reports will appear as separate worksheets and should match the Answer Report and Sensitivity Report in Exhibit 15.

The LP solution for Weston Company is provided below the Problem Setup in Exhibit 15. As you can see, the LP solution has identified Machine 2 as the process bottleneck and has calculated the maximum possible throughput values (sales prices minus the cost of direct materials times units sold) of the two products based on both the processing time and market constraints in the operation. The resulting optimal mix (100 hockey sticks and 36 baseball bats) is the same mix we computed earlier.

Notice also that the LP program has computed both the process slack and the market slack in the system. Machine 2 has no slack, which clearly indicates its status as the system bottleneck. In fact, profit will increase by $2.00 for every minute that Weston Company is able to increase the Machine 2 capacity beyond 2,400 minutes (see the shadow price in the Sensitivity Report in Exhibit 15). In addition, the zero market-demand slack for hockey sticks indicates that this market is currently satisfied. If Weston is able to obtain more processing time at Machine 2, then more baseball bats can be produced. In fact, see whether you can calculate how many more minutes of Machine 2 can be obtained before the bottleneck moves outside the organization to the market?[17]

---

[17] Answer: 50 bats demanded − 36 bats sold = 14 potential bat sales per week. 14 bats × 25 Machine 2 processing minutes = 350 more minutes needed. (This allowable increase on Machine 2 is displayed in the Sensitivity Report in Exhibit 15.)

Exhibit 15
Linear Programming Problem Setup

	A	B	C	D	E	F	G	H
1	**Data**							
2	Stick Price	$ 55.00						
3	Bat Price	$ 60.00			**Constraints**			
4	Stick RM Cost	$ 20.00			Minutes	Minutes	Total	
5	Bat RM Cost	$ 13.00			per Stick	per Bat	Minutes	Ceiling
6	Sticks Produced			Machine 1	10	5	-	2,400
7	Bats Produced			Machine 2	15	25	-	2,400
8				Machine 3	10	3	-	2,400
9	**Objective Function**			Assembly	20	2	-	2,400
10	Stick Revenue	$ -					Total	-
11	Bat Revenue	$ -			**Market Demand**			
12	Stick RM Cost	$ -		Sticks	100			
13	Bat RM Cost	$ -		Bats	50			
14	Throughput Value	$ -						
15	Operating Expenses	$(3,000)						
16	Profit	$(3,000)						

Linear Programming Answer Report

	B	C	D	E	F	G
6	Target Cell (Max)					
7	Cell	Name	Original Value	Final Value		
8	$B$16	Profit	$ (3,000)	$ 2,192		
11	Adjustable Cells					
12	Cell	Name	Original Value	Final Value		
13	$B$6	Sticks Produced	-	100		
14	$B$7	Bats Produced	-	36		
17	Constraints					
18	Cell	Name	Cell Value	Formula	Status	Slack
19	$G$6	Machine 1 Minutes	1,180	$G$6<=$H$6	Not Binding	1220
20	$G$7	Machine 2 Minutes	2,400	$G$7<=$H$7	Binding	0
21	$G$8	Machine 3 Minutes	1,108	$G$8<=$H$8	Not Binding	1292
22	$G$9	Assembly Minutes	2,072	$G$9<=$H$9	Not Binding	328
23	$B$6	Sticks Produced	100	$B$6<=$E$12	Binding	0
24	$B$7	Bats Produced	36	$B$7<=$E$13	Not Binding	14

Exhibit 15 (continued)
Linear Programming Sensitivity Report

	A	B	C	D	E	F	G	H
6	Adjustable Cells							
7				Final	Reduced	Objective	Allowable	Allowable
8		Cell	Name	Value	Cost	Coefficient	Increase	Decrease
9		$B$6	Sticks Produced	100	7	34.99999998	1E+30	6.799999983
10		$B$7	Bats Produced	36	-	47	11.3333333	47
11								
12	Constraints							
13				Final	Shadow	Constraint	Allowable	Allowable
14		Cell	Name	Value	Price	R.H. Side	Increase	Decrease
15		$G$6	Machine 1 Minutes	1,180	-	2400	1E+30	1220
16		$G$7	Machine 2 Minutes	2,400	2	2400	350	1E+30
17		$G$8	Machine 3 Minutes	1,108	-	2400	1E+30	1292
18		$G$9	Assembly Minutes	2,072	-	2400	1E+30	328

Critical Limitations of Linear Programming.

When comparing LP and TOC models, you should note that LP is strictly a mathematical formulation of a business setting. It is important to understand, however, that TOC (with the support of throughput accounting) is a comprehensive management tool that addresses many realities of process management that are difficult to incorporate within a strict mathematical model. For instance, the realities involved in applying constraint management include the following:

1. The dependence of operations on one another.
2. The potential for idle times on both constrained and unconstrained operations.
3. The need for buffer inventory stocks to manage dependencies and idle times within the system.

To be specific, simple LP mathematical models, such as the model shown in Exhibit 15, do not incorporate the fact that hockey sticks and baseball bats have to be produced in a particular sequence. For instance, the assembly operation at Weston Company is not a bottleneck, but it is highly dependent on all the proceeding operations. Hence it may be unnecessarily idle while waiting for another operation to complete its work on in-process inventory. In fact, the potential for excessive idle time at the assembly operation could actually create a real problem in the system. Notice in the LP solution in Exhibit 15 that assembly has only 328 minutes of slack. This slack time represents the total number of minutes that assembly can be idle during the week. Otherwise, the LP solution becomes invalid as the bottleneck shifts to the assembly operation.

Essentially, the challenge in using LP solutions is one of scheduling. Implementing the LP solution at Weston Company requires the use of buffer stocks and careful scheduling to avoid expensive idle time. The TOC management system addresses these issues using the drum-buffer-rope scheduling system.

The drum-buffer-rope concept of TOC is critical to implementing, managing, and realizing the solution described in Exhibits 12 and 15. Reconsider the production process at Weston Company as displayed in Exhibit 9. Clearly, Weston needs to establish a buffer of aluminum inventory in front of Machine 2 to ensure that fluctuations in ordering and receiving direct materials do not cause the bottleneck to be idle. Further, Weston needs to establish a good rope schedule with its aluminum supplier to ensure that aluminum is received in enough time to keep the buffer inventory from becoming either too large (expensive) or too small (risky). However, creating a production schedule (the drum) in the company that will keep the assembly operation from becoming a bottleneck is most critical.

Note in Exhibit 9 that each machine works on parts for both hockey sticks and baseball bats. Should Weston Company produce all 100 hockey sticks first and then produce the 36 baseball bats? Alternatively, should baseball bats be produced before hockey sticks? Is it best for the machines to alternate between producing bats and sticks? Determining the correct production order prevents assembly from exceeding its slack time limits and impeding Weston's goal of producing 100 hockey sticks and 36 baseball bats each week.

What if Weston decides to produce 36 baseball bats before beginning production on the 100 hockey sticks? Do you see how it will take 25 minutes for the baseball bat work-in-process inventory to arrive at assembly (Machine 2 works for 15 minutes on a shaft and then for 10 minutes on a handle cover)? Once the in-process inventory arrives, assembly works for two minutes to complete the baseball bat. Assembly must then wait for 23 minutes before it has the materials needed to assemble another bat.[18] Hence producing 36 bats will result in approximately 828 minutes of idle time in the assembly operation (36 bats x 23 minutes per bat idle time). Remember that the LP solution in Exhibit 15 indicates that assembly has only 328 minutes in idle time available. Producing all the baseball bats first will not allow enough time for Weston to complete production of 100 hockey sticks. The amount of overtime required when Machine 2 is dedicated to producing only baseball bats clearly suggests that Weston cannot simply switch the production schedule to produce the 100 hockey sticks before producing the 36 baseball bats.

What if Weston decides to rotate production of hockey sticks and baseball bats on Machine 2 (the bottleneck operation)? Specifically, Weston will use Machine 2 to produce a hockey stick and then use Machine 2 to produce a baseball bat. In this manner, assembly will be able to switch back and forth, assembling hockey sticks and then baseball bats. This idea makes sense because assembly may be able to use idle time waiting for baseball bats to assemble hockey sticks. Testing this potential schedule (a challenge requiring a complicated simulation analysis either in Excel™ or in some other software program) is beyond the purposes of this module. Nevertheless, a separate analysis of this proposal reveals that Weston would able to produce all 36 bats using this schedule. However, the end of the week would arrive just as assembly begins work on about the 85th hockey stick.

It appears that the LP solution is invalid. In fact, because of interdependencies of operations and potential idle times, LP-based solutions for some processes are not valid. However, further study reveals a number of potential scheduling solutions that will allow the Weston to produce all 100 hockey sticks and 36 baseball bats. Successfully implementing one of these schedules requires the management of buffer inventories and careful adherence to the drum production schedule by all non-bottleneck operations in the system.

In contrast to TOC, LP does not act as a management tool. Determining the mathematical solution to a constraint problem is one thing; implementing that solution into an actual organization is an entirely different matter. With throughput accounting as its information system, TOC uses the five-step model to implement a solution to process constraints and then manages the process with the drum-buffer-rope system.

---

[18] Assembly has to wait only 23 minutes (rather than 25 minutes), since Machine 2 began working on a new bat while Assembly completed the current bat.

▲ COMMON TERMS

Activity   The series of related tasks that are part of work performed in an organization. It represents what is done such as the several things needed to load a truck with goods to be shipped, or responding to a customer complaint. (See Process diagram.)

Activity-Based Costing (ABC)   A method of costing in which activities are the primary cost objects. ABC measures cost and performance of activities and assigns the costs of those activities to other cost objects, such as products or customers, based on their use of activities.

Allocation   The apportionment or distribution of a common cost between two or more cost objects. In accounting, allocation is usually a way of assigning a cost between cost objects (products, departments or processes) that share that common cost. An allocation involves dividing the cost needed to allocate by some physical quantity (ideally a cost driver).

Benchmarking   The process of investigating and identifying "best practices" and using them as a standard to improve one's own processes and activities.

Budget   A quantitative plan of action that helps an organization coordinate resource inflows and outflows for a specific time period. Budgets are usually financial but may also include nonfinancial operating information.

Capacity   The physical facilities, personnel, supplier contacts, and processes necessary to meet the product or service needs of customers.

Cost   A monetary measure of the resources consumed by a product, service, function, or activity. It also refers to the price paid for acquiring a product or service.

Cost Driver   An event or factor that has a systematic relationship to a particular type of cost and causes that cost to be incurred.

Cost Management   The systematic analysis of cost drivers for the purpose of understanding how to reduce or maintain costs.

Cost Object   Any item (activity, customer, project, work unit, product, channel, or service) for which a measurement of cost is desired.

Competitive Analysis   Tools that enable companies to quantify how performance and costs compare against competitors, understand why performance and costs are different, and apply that insight to strengthen competitive responses and implement proactive plans.

Continuous Improvement   A program to improve the strategic variables of quality, cost or time in small incremental steps on a continuous basis.

Culture   The collective values, beliefs, ethics, and mindsets of the members of an organization, clan, or society which is subconsciously used to interpret events and take action. It is often called the collective programming of the subconscious mind.

Extended Enterprise   The extended enterprise includes an organization's customers, suppliers, dealers, and recyclers. It captures the interdependencies across these separate organizations. It is also referred to as the value chain.

Fixed Cost   A cost element that does not vary with changes in production volume in the short-run. The property taxes on a factory building is an example of a fixed production cost.

Incremental Cost   1. The cost associated with increasing the output of an activity or project above some base level. 2. The additional cost associated with selecting one economic or business alternative over another, such as difference between working overtime or subcontracting the work.

Indirect Costs   Costs that are not directly assignable or traceable to a cost object.

Life-Cycle Costs   Accumulation of costs for activities that occur over the entire life cycle of a product from inception to abandonment.

Process   A series of linked activities that perform a specific objective. A process has a beginning, an end, and clearly identified inputs and outputs.

Process

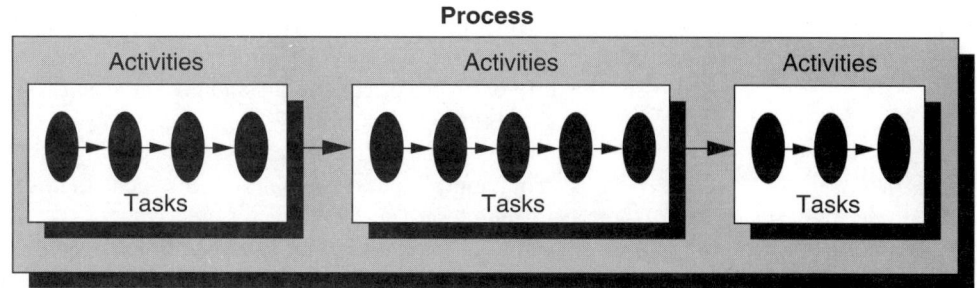

Quality   A customer's total experience with a product or service. It includes features and the performance dimensions of those features such as reliability, usability, safety, and repairability.

Strategy   The way that an organization positions and differentiates itself from its competitors. Positioning refers to the selection of target customers. Distinctions typically are made on the dimensions of quality, cost, and time.

Time   The time it takes a firm to develop and produce new products or to provide existing products when customers need them.

Value Chain   (See Extended Enterprise.)

Variable Cost   A cost element that varies directly and proportionately with changes in production volume.

▲ PROBLEMS AND CASES

1. Self-test questions.

a. Define a constraint and list several factors that can cause fluctuations in production.
b. List the three bases of competition for an organization that may be challenged by constraints and process fluctuations. Describe a potential problem for each.
c. What is the drum-buffer-rope system? Describe the function of the three components and discuss the importance of each.
d. What are the five steps in the TOC process?
e. List the different types of constraints and give at least two examples of each.
f. How does one elevate a constraint?
g. Is it possible to be free from constraints? Why or why not?
h. What is throughput accounting? Where is the focus in this type of accounting (short term, long term, etc.)?
i. How does TOC define throughput and operational expense? How is this different from the traditional accounting definitions?
j. Can throughput-focused statements be used for GAAP purposes? Explain.
k. What are some of the possible consequences of piling up work-in-process inventory?
l. Should GAAP-based statements be used for managerial purposes? Explain.
m. How can slack time be beneficially used in a "lean" manufacturing situation?
n. What are the two main technical aspects of TOC accounting, and how can an organization benefit from them?
o. What are the four critical behavioral aspects of TOC accounting, and why are they critical?
p. What adjustments are necessary to an organization's culture for TOC accounting to be successful?

Short Exercises.

2. Risenmight Woodcrafters, Inc., manufactures desks. Each desk sells for $400 and contains materials totaling $100. Salaries, insurance, and payroll taxes are $750, supplies expense is $200, and miscellaneous expenses are $2,200. Risenmight sells 50 desks.

Required:
Calculate throughput, operating expense, and profit for Risenmight.

3. "I thought JIT was the way of the future," Paulo grumbled as he looked down at the production floor that he managed. "But we still have piles of inventory building . . . no matter how hard we try to eliminate them!" Swen, Paulo's assistant manager, racked his brain for a solution that had not yet been tried. Then he remembered a conversation he had with Kjirsten, the division manager, at the last division meeting. "Paulo, do you remember Kjiersten talking about that book . . . *The Goal*?" Swen asked. "Yes, something about bottlenecks and drums. What about it?" "I think she might be able to help us solve our inventory problem."

Required:
As Kjiersten, explain to Paulo and Swen why JIT may not be working in their plant. Be sure to explain the merits of JIT, as well as compare and contrast JIT and TOC.

4. "Anya, we have to manage our inventory better!" Trevon, plant manager at Durhamite Co., said to one of the floor supervisors. These high levels of inventory have to be hurting our profitability. We are not concentrating on throughput."

"Well," Anya replied, "I talked to Collin in accounting, and he showed me the numbers—look. Our sales are constant at 40 units a month, and for the last three months we have produced 40, 50, and 80 units. Our revenue is $2,800 per unit, our materials costs are $1,000 per unit, and our conversion costs are stable at $80,000 per month. The numbers work out so that we do better, profitwise, when we increase inventory."

Required:

As Anya, prove to Trevon (by preparing a GAAP-based P&L statement) that building inventory is profitable. As Trevon, prove to Anya that building inventory is detrimental to Durhamite. Prepare a P&L statement based on throughput and explain the contradiction with GAAP-based results. Assume that selling, general, and administrative expenses are constant at $7,500 per month.

5. Classify the following as process, policy, material, or market constraints. In addition, categorize each constraint as internal or external.

a. Oil embargo.

b. Freeze on overtime.

c. A false press report curtails consumer desire for the product.

d. A key bank service starts becoming obsolete.

e. Consumers are unaware of a product's capability.

f. Company restrictions on equipment purchases.

g. One machine works slower than the rest.

h. Parts must be treated before they can be installed.

i. Frost in Florida (to an orange juice producer).

j. Management has preestablished batch sizes on all machines.

k. Extensive special training is required to work on certain types of consulting contracts.

l. State regulations limit the number of driving hours for heavy-equipment operators.

m. Union contracts strictly limit the categories of equipment that workers can operate.

6. Why do we need all these different accounting systems? Marcus asked himself as he left the accounting department of Ohrano Theater Supply, Inc. As manager of the production floor, Marcus is responsible for providing the accounting department with the monthly figures from his department. He had just learned that Ohrano was going to implement a new constraint management system, and he now has to keep track of even more numbers than before. He decided to talk to Marina, Ohrano's controller, to see whether there was a simpler way. All this number chasing is taking away from his time on the floor.

Required:

As Marina, convince Marcus that one system is not a replacement for the other. Explain the differences between throughput accounting and conventional accounting, as well as the needs for each.

7. "You mean to tell me that these machines are supposed to just sit there?!! And those machine operators—what do they do while their machine is down for two hours?" Jake Michaels, plant supervisor for GreenCo, was meeting with the vice-president of production, Karen Wendell. Wendell had been assigned by the board of directors to implement TOC in production—starting with Michaels' plant. So far, it was not going well.

Required:

As Karen Wendell, explain to Jake Michaels why it is not beneficial to have all resources operating at full capacity. Provide some alternative performance measures that can replace the traditional efficiency variances.

8.

Pizanno Enterprises
GAAP-Based P&L Statement
For the Month of January 2001

Sales Revenue		$100,000
Cost of Goods Sold		(50,000)
Gross Margin		$50,000
Period Costs		
Selling Costs	$15,000	
Gen. Admin. Costs	20,000	
Total Period Costs		(35,000)
OPERATING INCOME		$15,000

Additional Information:

a. Sold 1,000 units (assume inventory levels and product costs per unit are constant between the current month and last month).
b. Cost of Goods Sold includes direct materials costs of $25 per unit, direct labor costs of $10 per unit labor, variable overhead of $5 per unit, and total fixed overhead of $10,000.
c. Other than a 5 percent commission on sales revenues, selling costs are all fixed.
d. General Administrative costs are 80 percent fixed.

Required:

Prepare a P&L statement following traditional contribution margin format. Prepare a second P&L statement according to TOC concepts.

9. Li Teng, CEO of Xing Xin Information Systems Consulting Group, has recently implemented TOC in his company. As soon as the program began, Li realized that the traditional performance measures were no longer consistent with company goals.

    Xing Xin specializes in database system installation. A typical engagement consists of six major tasks as follows:

1. Establish specific needs of client.
2. Analyze current system.
3. Design new system.
4. Implement new system.

5. Transfer old data to new system.

6. Test and evaluate new system.

Through TOC, Li discovered the process bottleneck at step 5. Only one of Xing Xin's consultants, Yinlien Zhou, is qualified to test new systems. Hence, Yinlien must be involved in step 6 for all client engagements. In addition, Yinlien has her own clients with whom she works throughout the engagement.

Required:

Devise some performance measures that will improve throughput performance at Xing Xin. Also give recommendations as to what can be done to increase the effectiveness of the system installation process.

10. DoubleSet Company is a manufacturing organization that produces two products, Trinidad and Maser. The manufacturing process for each product is basically a two-step operation involving three employees. Bob performs a preliminary manufacturing step on Machine A for each of the two products produced in the DoubleSet Company. It takes him five minutes to complete a product on Machine A. Naomi then operates Machine B for 20 minutes to complete each Trinidad product. Similarly, Luis operates Machine C for 20 minutes to complete each Maser product. All three employees work eight-hour days. Thus, they each have 480 minutes of daily processing time available to them (8 hours × 60 minutes). Assume now that both products provide $100 of throughput per product. The table below describes the setup necessary to perform an LP solution for DoubleSet Company.

			Minutes per Trinidad	Minutes per Maser	Total Minutes	Daily Ceiling
Trinidads produced						
Masers produced						
Trinidad throughput	$100	Machine A	5	5		480
Maser throughput	$100	Machine B	20	0		480
Total throughput		Machine C	0	20		480

Required:

Input the data above into an LP software such as Microsoft Excel™ and compute the optimal answer and sensitivity analysis. Identify the bottleneck(s) from the LP solution.

11. For each of the following situations, answer these three questions:

a. What is a likely constraint in this situation?

b. How would you manage this costraint using a buffer, a rope schedule, and a drum schedule?

c. How might you elevate the constraint?

Situation 1: Issuing drivers' licenses at the county traffic office (think about how the process worked when you received your first driver's license).

Situation 2: Compiling tax returns for clients at a local H&R Block company (compiling client tax returns includes operations such as client meetings, record compilations, and work review by supervisors).

Situation 3: Teaching long division to a class of eight-year-olds (assume the general procedure is to teach the class, individually work with students, assess the class, and work with the remaining students who do not adequately understand the material).

Comprehensive problems.

12. Bogeeta, Inc., manufactures two products—bicycles and skateboards.[19] For each bicycle sold, the company receives $95. For each skateboard sold, it receives $65. Each bicycle requires 10 minutes of Gordy's time, 15 minutes of Kelly's time, 8 minutes of David's time, and 10 minutes of Beckie's time. Each skateboard requires 10 minutes from Gordy, 20 minutes from Kelly, 15 minutes from David, and 20 minutes from Beckie. Each worker at Bogeeta works 40 hours per week, and no overtime is allowed. Raw materials cost $40 for each bicycle manufactured and $25 for each skateboard. Demand is unlimited, as is the supply of raw materials. Factory overhead for the plant is $6,000 per week, including the wages for Gordy, Kelly, David, and Beckie.

Required:

How many bicycles and skateboards should Bogeeta manufacture this week assuming there is unlimited demand for bicycles and skateboards? What is the optimal profit provided by this schedule?

13. Consider the Bogeeta, Inc., manufacturing situation presented in the preceding problem. Assume that the production requirements for its two products—bicycles and skateboards—are unchanged. However, assume that Bogeeta is able to sell only 110 bicycles and 50 skateboards each week. Further, Bogeeta's marketing manager has recently received a request from an exporter to purchase all the bicycles the company can provide at a reduced price of $50.00 per bike. Since these bicycles will be shipped overseas, the sale to the exporter will not affect Bogeeta's current local market demand of 110 bicycles weekly.

Required:

Part 1: Before considering the overseas bid for a special purchase, compute the optimal solution for Bogeeta given the limited local market demand for bicycles and skateboards. What is the net profit of the firm with this strategy?

Part 2: In light of your solution to Part 1, analyze the overseas bid. Should the company accept the bid? If Bogeeta accepts, how many bicycles should be produced for domestic sales, how many bicycles should be produced for the exporter, and how many skateboards should be produced? What is the net profit of the firm with this new strategy?

14. Part 1: The Rochester plant manufactures three miniature television products that are distinguished by their screen sizes: 3, 5, and 6 inches. Market demand over the next week, unit sales prices, and costs of direct materials per unit are provided in the following diagram. Weekly labor costs are estimated to be $62,000. Weekly manufacturing overhead costs are budgeted at $130,000. Selling and general administrative costs are $75,000 each week. Rochester runs a 80-hour work week (two 40-hour shifts per week) and tries not to schedule any facilities to work overtime.

---

[19] The authors gratefully acknowledge material provided by Professor Sid Sytsma of Ferris State University in the preparation of Problems 12, 13, and 14.

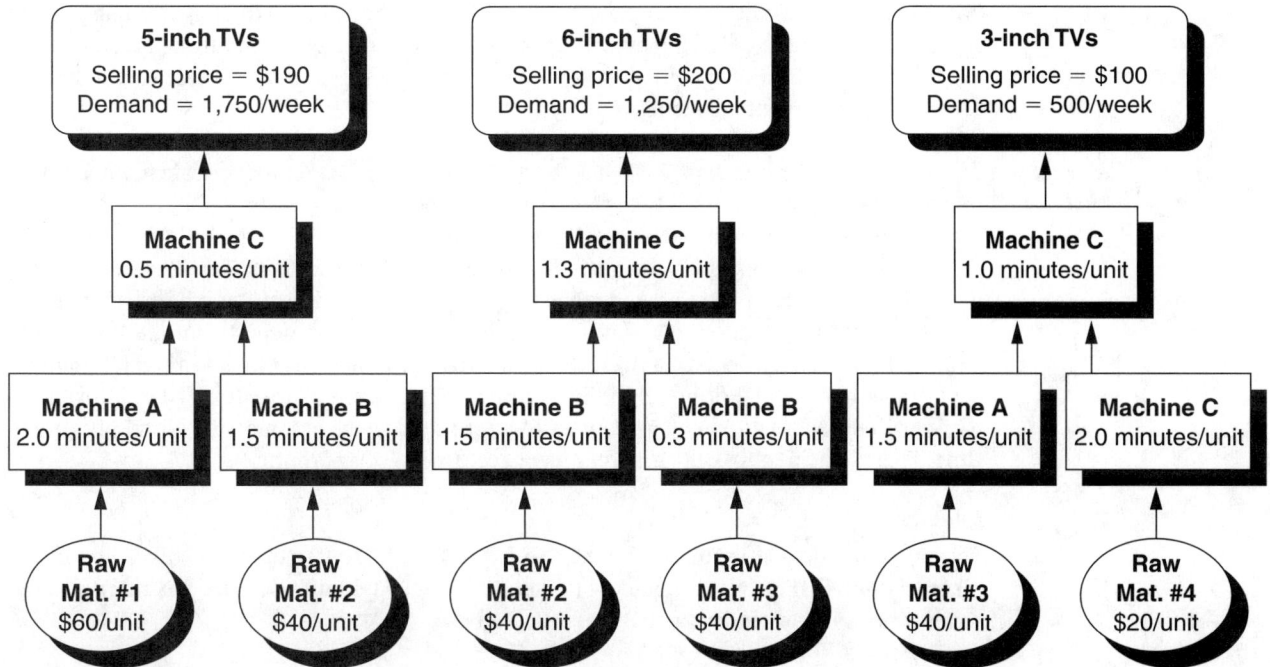

5-inch TVs	6-inch TVs	3-inch TVs
Selling price = $190	Selling price = $200	Selling price = $100
Demand = 1,750/week	Demand = 1,250/week	Demand = 500/week

Machine C	Machine C	Machine C
0.5 minutes/unit	1.3 minutes/unit	1.0 minutes/unit

Machine A	Machine B	Machine B	Machine B	Machine A	Machine C
2.0 minutes/unit	1.5 minutes/unit	1.5 minutes/unit	0.3 minutes/unit	1.5 minutes/unit	2.0 minutes/unit

Raw Mat. #1 $60/unit	Raw Mat. #2 $40/unit	Raw Mat. #2 $40/unit	Raw Mat. #3 $40/unit	Raw Mat. #3 $40/unit	Raw Mat. #4 $20/unit

Required:

Determine the optimal production mix to maximize profit over the next week at Rochester.

Part 2: Assume that the production mix you establish in Part 1 is achieved over the next week. As a result of realistic issues involving production sequencing and scheduling, actual operating minutes for each machine during the one-week period are as follows:

	Machine A	**Machine B**	**Machine C**
Actual Operating Minutes (for two weeks)	4,572 minutes	4,856 minutes	4,402 minutes

Required:

First calculate an efficiency variance for each machine using the following formula:

Total actual production in units
× Standard minutes per unit
Total standard minutes allowed
− Total actual minutes
Efficiency Variance

Plant management at Rochester is concerned that each machine should always be operating at peak efficiency. Management is also concerned about the fact that Machines A and C are not operating at their capacity of 4,800 minutes per week (i.e., they appear to have excess capacity). Using your insight regarding how TOC is used to separately manage bottleneck and non-bottleneck operations, how would you help the Rochester management adjust its assessment of each machine operation to be consistent with throughput accounting? Be sure to discuss specifically how to interpret the efficiency variance calculated on each machine, as well any excess capacity.

15. Fashionable Bikes, Inc. (FBI) has the hottest new product on the upscale toy market—high quality boys' and girls' bikes in bright fashion colors. Due to a seller's market for high-quality toys for the newest baby boomers, FBI can sell bikes at the following throughput margins: boys' bikes—$30, girls' bikes—$50. To maintain market share focus, the marketing department recommends that at least 250 bikes of each type be produced per day. A boy's bike requires four labor hours in the fabrication department and one labor hour in the assembly department. A girl's bike requires four labor hours in the fabrication department and two labor hours in the assembly department. Currently, FBI employs 200 workers in the fabrication department and 100 workers in the assembly department in each shift. There are three 8-hour shifts per day (overtime is not permitted).

Required:

Formulate the preceding information as an LP problem. How many boys' bikes and girls' bikes should FBI produce per day to maximize throughput? Be sure to interpret any shadow prices reported by the LP software you use.

16. The U.S. Patent Office receives literally millions of requests each year to issue patents on various inventions that may be generally classified into four categories:

- ▲ *Machines* such as engines or tools.
- ▲ *Manufactured items* such as kitchen utensils or window sun shades.
- ▲ *Matter composition* such as fertilizer or toothpaste.
- ▲ *Processes* such as methods of preparing synthetic proteins.

Analyzing these patents is typically a twofold process involving application examination and patent search. The process of application examination is done essentially to determine whether the invention is *useful and nonobvious*. For example, a pen that writes in lime-green ink is probably too obvious to pass the application examination process. In addition to the examination, a patent search process is completed to determine that the inventions is *novel*. That is, an invention must be reasonably distinct from previous patents filed at the U.S. Patent Office.

Assume, for example, that inventions involving *machines* generally require two hours to complete an application examination and three hours to complete a patent search. Conversely, application examinations and patent searches on *processes* require three hours and two hours, respectively. Assume also that the U.S. Patent Office employs a specialist to handle the examination process and a database researcher trained to perform the patent searches on machines and processes. The weekly salary for the examination specialist is $1,200, and the weekly salary for a database researcher is $1,000. Each of these two professionals is available 40 hours per week. Finally, given that there is always a backlog of applications and that a high percentage of applications are rejected by the U.S. Patent Office, the management has determined that patent searches and application examinations

---

[20] Problem adapted from R. Verma, "My Operations Management Students Love Linear Programming," *Decision Line* (July 1997): 9–12.

must be carefully managed. Hence, in order to not waste the more expensive time of the specialist, the researcher always completes the patent search before handing off the application to the specialist for the application examination. Overall, the goal is to maximize the number of patents getting through the system each week in a context where professionals employed in the U.S. Patent Office do not work more than 40 hours per week.

Required:
1. Set up and solve this constraint using standard LP procedures.
2. Consider carefully whether the LP solution you generated is valid. What is the effect of having the researcher perform his work before the specialist is allowed to begin her work on the patent application? Would it affect the validity of your LP solution if management decided to reverse the processing order to require that the examination specialist had to complete her work before the researcher could begin his work on the application?
3. Provide some type of "what if" analysis to numerically demonstrate your position on the issue of scheduling effects on the LP solution.

Team projects.

For each of the organizational scenarios listed as team projects, discuss and determine the following questions as a group:

a. What is the goal of the organization?
b. What constraints exist? Classify each constraint.
c. How can you be sure that the critical constraint has been identified?
d. What data is needed to implement TOC?
e. What type of information would a throughput accounting system provide to measure organization's progress toward the goal?
f. What additional information and performance measures will be needed to support implementation of TOC in this scenario?

1. Organizational Scenario: The hub of a major airline.
2. Organizational Scenario: A community church or synagogue.
3. Organizational Scenario: A commercial building construction company.

Case 1: The Denver Drive Company.[21]

The Denver Drive Company is an established producer of large hard drives for use in commercial computers. Hard drives are produced in large quantities for delivery to large-scale computer assemblers or to computer parts distributors. Despite the presence of a "middle-man" between the company and the ultimate end user of its product (e.g., commercial customers purchasing its hard drive units or purchasing computers containing its hard drive units), Denver Drive directly guarantees the reliability of its product.

The repair division.
The top-of-the-line drives produced by Denver Drive are typically based on the SCSI interface except for a small number that are manufactured with a proprietary interface. Basically, a disk drive consists of two major subassemblies:

---

[21] The authors gratefully acknowledge field-research material provided by James W. Kwiecien in the preparation of this case.

1. A head disk assembly or HDA. This assembly contains the drive motor, the heads, the disks, the actuator, and preamps. HDAs are very precise devices and must be assembled in a climate-controlled clean room to avoid any contamination that might later cause a head crash.

2. A circuit board that controls the functioning of the drive and allows it to communicate with the controller card in the computer. Given that these are high-end drives, the circuit board is powerful enough that if you simply added a keyboard, video output, and some RAM, you would have a basic computer.

Based on the highly technical nature of hard drive manufacturing, it is expected that customers will experience a small number of drive failures. As a result of Denver Drive's commitment to its customers, a dedicated repair operation was established to handle all hard drive returns. With the increasing number of drive shipments, even the tiny percentage of drives that failed soon resulted in significant levels of returns. To manage the costs of supporting the hard drive product, the terms of the warranty offered to its customers allowed replacement of failed drives with repaired and refurbished, rather than brand new, units. Also, the large number of good drives with which no problem could be found provided a financial incentive to scale up the screening and repair process. Additionally, the failure modes experienced usually resulted in a defective HDA mated with a perfectly good board, or vice versa. To discard good components just because they were mated with a defective part would not make financial sense in an industry characterized by razor-thin profit margins.

To build motivation and discipline, Denver Drive executive management used transfer pricing to establish the repair division as a profit center in the company. For every driver actually repaired in the division, it was "paid" $200. For drives determined to be NTF (that is, No Trouble Found) and simply tested and shipped back to the customer, the division received $75. Monthly operating costs (including costs of all employees) is approximately $175,000.

Failure analysis.
Hard drive failures, as reported by customers, can be categorized as one of four types (approximate percentage of instances are also noted):

1. HDA Failure—25 percent.
2. Board Failure—25 percent.
3. HDA and Board Failure—15 percent.
4. No Trouble Found—35 percent.

Failure analysis is important so that designs could be refined and future failures reduced. It was also found that many failures are customer induced, rather than being rooted in the drive itself. For example, the customer may have dropped the drive or subjected it to electrostatic discharge. In other cases, when customers had problems integrating the drive into a system, they would attempt to fix the drive themselves, sometimes even opening the HDA without the benefit of a clean room. Sometimes a drive model would not function properly with a customer's firmware, and in some instances customers just did not know what they were doing. It was also not unknown for a customer to find out that a new revision to his or her drive had been introduced and purposely damage the existing drive so it could be returned for replacement by the latest and greatest model.

The initial repair process.
The initial repair process was originally centered around experienced disk drive repair technicians. Most of these people have been working with disk drives for years and are

intimately familiar with disk drive operating characteristics and failure modes. The basic analysis and repair process was as follows:

▲ Disk drive arrives, is checked against outstanding repair and maintenance agreements, and is entered into the database. At this point the drive is inspected for misuse or physical damage.

▲ Technicians are scheduled to work on specific drive models by production control.

▲ Technician diagnoses drive.

▲ If no problem is found with the drive (i.e., NTF status), it is sent forward to have test code loaded into memory.

▲ If the technician diagnoses a board problem, the drive is sent another department to have the board replaced by a lower-level employee. After board replacement, the referring technician again diagnoses the drive.

▲ If the technician diagnoses an HDA problem, the board is removed and the HDA sent, along with repair instructions provided by the technician, to the clean room for rework on the read/write head, platter, or actuator. Alternatively, the technician may send the HDA to the non-clean room for repair work such as redoing the servo writing on the unit. When the HDA rework and repair is completed, it is mated up with an available board and retested.

▲ Once the technician feels that the drive is functioning properly, it is sent forward to have test code loaded into memory. If it fails to properly accept and hold the test code, it is returned to the technician for more diagnostic work.

▲ The drive is then mounted on a large computer cabinet where it tests and calibrates itself using the test code. This test can take from 12 to 40 hours to complete depending on the performance level and capacity of the drive. Currently the division has three self-test cabinets (each cabinet holds 70 units).

▲ If the drive passes the self-test and calibration on the cabinet, it is sent forward to be loaded with customer code. If it fails to properly accept and hold the customer's code, it is returned to the technician for further diagnostic work.

▲ After being loaded with customer code, the drive is labeled, packaged, and shipped back to the customer.

Other than new circuit boards, there is actually very little substantive materials cost in the repair process. The repair division is charged $50 for each circuit board it uses.

The initial efforts to increase production at the repair division.
The initial repair process described above was slow, inefficient, and expensive. The 21 technicians were able to process through an average of two drives per day, four if they were lucky. Turnaround times were so long that often the products became obsolete before they could be repaired and returned to the customer (this obviously was a source of constant irritation between Denver Drive Company and its customers). Average shipments ranged between 30 and 50 units a week. The backlog of drives waiting for technician analysis sometimes ranged as high as 1,000 units. Hence the repair division sometimes purchased new drives from the manufacturing division for emergency replacements for priority customers. Since the production line was straining to fill new customer orders, this practice sometimes had major effects on the company's ability to meet production schedules.

It was at this point that Todd Kinney was hired as a specialist to work on the problems in the repair process at Denver Drive. His initial assignment was to hire more technicians. He did, and output went up a bit, just a little bit. The learning curve for new technicians proved to be very steep. Throwing people at the process just did not increase output very much. Further, the monthly cost to employ a technician was $3,200. A new engineering manager for the division was transferred in from another division to work with Todd. The new engineering manager was serious about improving production.

It was obvious to Todd and the engineering manager that one of the division's problems, in large part due to the circular nature of the process, was the flow of units under repair. The engineering manager decided that this was a major problem (it was) and that they should revisit the layout of the production area to improve efficiency. Todd was given the responsibility of getting it done and was removed from his fire-fighting role so he could take a closer look at the process. Although he inherited the mindset that the technicians were the key to the process, after a few days of observation and study, Todd realized that there were really two bottlenecks in the system. The obvious one was the technicians. The other one was the self-test and calibration process. Every time a technician diagnosed a drive, it would eventually end up at the test cabinets. These cabinets occasionally fell behind the analysis and repair process. Hence, even if Todd and the division manager could substantially increase the output from the technicians, the three self-test cabinets were insufficient to handle an increased volume of units. This situation reminded Todd of a book he had intended to read several years earlier, *The Goal* by Eliyahu Goldratt and Jeff Fox. He went home that night and started reading the book.

Required:

1. Create a diagram of the initial repair process based on the preceding description. Does Todd Kinney appear to have a reasonable grasp of the constraint issues in this process?

2. Using the transfer price and cost data in the case, try to reasonably piece together some type of a monthly throughput margin P&L statement for the current process. You will likely need to make some approximations and assumptions here.

3. Consider the five-step TOC process (identify the constraint, exploit the constraint, subordinate all non-constraint operations, elevate the constraint, and identify the next constraint). The first step is already illustrated in the case. If you were Todd Kinney, how might you redesign the repair process to exploit, subordinate, and elevate?

4. Create a new diagram of the repair process that incorporates your ideas.

5. In light of the bottleneck operation(s) you have identified and attempted to exploit and elevate, how would you identify performance measures to subordinate non-bottleneck operations? Would performance measures need to be different for an operation that was upstream versus downstream from the bottleneck operation(s)? Why?

6. Assume that you must now present your recommendation to the controller for Denver Drive Company. This controller is an excellent accountant, but is not trained in TOC or throughput accounting. What objections might the controller have to your solution? How would you convince the controller that your solution is optimal despite some of the negative performance measures it could generate in a traditional budget system?

Case 2: Lindo's Restaurant.

"Well," thought Danilo Rictor, "I guess we find out tonight if all that work is going to pay off." Danilo stepped out of the backroom that he uses as his office, took one last turn around the his restaurant, and gave some final instructions to the line chief in the kitchen before stepping out to help the host greet some early dinner guests.

Lindo's is a favorite local restaurant offering a standard menu of southwestern cuisine. In the 12 years since it first opened its doors, Lindo's has become one of the more popular restaurants in the city. Danilo Rictor, the restaurant's owner/manager, has built a successful business around a tasteful menu and a firm policy of absolute customer service and satisfaction. In addition, Danilo focuses a lot of attention on making sure his staff is happy and enjoying their work. Paying his servers and kitchen workers a bit more than the market wage rate helps. However, Danilo found that the real key to employing an effective and enthusiastic staff is to provide good training, allow workers to manage themselves whenever possible, and create excitement with frequent productivity contests.

Essentially, there are two categories of employees at Lindo's—the guest staff and the kitchen staff. The guest staff includes hosts, servers, expediters, cashiers, and busers. Hosts greet the guests, assign seating, and introduce the server. Servers take orders, deliver food and beverages, and take care of guest payments. Expeditors stand ready to assist servers. If tables need to be rearranged, if large trays of food need to be delivered, or if the server falls behind in any way, an expeditor is expected to jump in and assist. Cashiers prepare the guest invoice (i.e., the check) for the servers. Servers then return with guest payments, and cashiers enter payments into the register and prepare the receipts. Busers clear and prepare the table after guests depart and then notify the hosts when tables are available.

The kitchen staff includes preparers, line cooks, fajita cooks, restockers, and dishwashers. Preparers work from 6:00 A.M. to 11:00 A.M. each day to complete most of the food preparation work. Preparers make ready large containers of fresh sides and garnishes such as chopped lettuce, grated cheese, and sliced tomatoes. More important, preparers create most of the entrees (main dishes) and hot appetizers. These items (such as enchiladas, burritos, and rellenos) are cooked to near completion and placed in a large walk-in cooler. One dishwasher works along with the preparers to ensure that the kitchen is in order when the rest of the kitchen staff begins arriving at 11:00 A.M. to service the day's customers, beginning with the lunch crowd. The process of servicing customer orders revolves around the three line cooks, with one of the line cooks acting as kitchen supervisor. Servers bring orders from the customers to the kitchen, and the line cooks fill the orders by removing appetizers and entrees from the cooler and quickly finishing the cooking process in large ovens. Fajita's cannot be precooked effectively. Hence, a fajita cook is dedicated to assembling all fajita orders as they come to the kitchen. As hot food items are completed, they are garnished with cold items (such as lettuce, tomatoes, and sauce). Two restockers stand ready in the kitchen to ensure that all the fresh sides and garnishes are available to the line cooks. In addition, restockers are in charge of preparing all sodas and specialty drinks ordered by customers. (Lindo's does not have a liquor license and, therefore, a bartender is not employed.) Three dishwashers work with the rest of the staff to keep clean utensils and dishes available to the rest of the kitchen staff.

As a result of Danilo's focus on customers and his successful work with his staff, Lindo's weekday lunch hours and weekend evenings are extremely busy. Analysis of the revenue flows indicates that 80 percent of revenues comes into the restaurant during these time periods. Hence, effective management of revenue resources is critical to improving profits. It is clear to Danilo and his management accountant that table turnover (measured as the number of tables cleared by the staff and available for guest seating each hour) is an important indicator that guests are being served promptly and that limited seating is being used effectively to generate restaurant revenue. Danilo's management accountant identified five critical operations in the process of serving the guest: (1) greeting and seating, (2) order taking, (3) dinner service, (4) check and payment, and (5) table cleanup and preparation.

It is clear to Danilo that there are a number of potential constraints on getting guests served. Danilo recently read *The Goal* as the result of attending an executive lecture at the local community college. He involved his chef, his head server, and the supervising receptionist to help him implement a TOC system at Lindo's. After quite a bit of effort, Danilo's team was able to make some significant improvements in the business. The results of their efforts to implement the five-step TOC process are as follows:

1. *Identify the constraint.* Danilo and his management accountant were able to quickly identify the line cooks as the bottleneck in the operation. The constant pile of unfulfilled orders in front of the kitchen during the lunch hour and on weekend evenings, coupled with frequent complaints from customers about wait time, made this first TOC step rather obvious.

2. *Exploit the constraint.* Hiring and training more line cooks is difficult and expensive to do. Besides, Danilo was convinced that he should first fully exploit this constraint before spending a lot of money to elevate it with additional line cooks staff. By involving the line cooks in the analysis, Danilo learned that they were often forced to wait because the restockers did not have garnish and side items available. A little more analysis revealed that restockers were spending too much time working on specialty drinks and did not pay enough attention to supporting the line cooks. Some training and new kitchen policies were enough to keep the critical line cooks constantly busy.

3. *Subordinate all nonconstraint processes.* Danilo's management accountant set up a drum-buffer-rope schedule to emphasize the importance of the line cook operation. It was quite clear to the accountant that endlessly piling up lunch and dinner orders in front of the line cooks was, at least, pointless and too often resulted in confusion in the kitchen. With a little experimentation, an appropriate buffer of kitchen orders was established to ensure that line cooks were not overwhelmed without risking unnecessary down time. A rope scheduling system was established to hold back the servers from bringing in orders too fast to the kitchen. Essentially, the kitchen would turn on a small subtle light in the restaurant to indicate that its buffer was full. When the light was on, servers were expected to slow down the flow of orders by using free specialty drinks to keep the seated customers happy. When the light was off, servers were free to bring orders to the kitchen. A drum system was established to ensure that an order never sat undelivered for more than one or two minutes once it was ready. The signal for this system was the presence of prepared orders on the order-out counter. Because servers could be anywhere in the restaurant when the kitchen completed an order, the expediters were assigned ultimate responsibility to watch this signal. If orders were ready, expeditors were expected to serve. This drum system eventually required a small increase in the number of scheduled expediters during busy times.

4. *Elevate the constraint.* Once the capacity of the line cooks had been fully exploited and all non-bottleneck operations completely subordinated to the needs of the line cooks, Danilo found it unnecessary to elevate the kitchen capacity. Even during the busiest times, Lindo's always served its guests promptly.

5. *Identify the next constraint.* With the kitchen process now optimally working, Danilo and his management accountant thought their TOC efforts were completed. However, Danilo continued to be bothered by the all-too-familiar backlog of guests waiting to be seated for the business lunch hour and for weekend dinner. The result of kitchen process improvement further enhanced the reputation of Lindo's, creating an even larger demand for seating during critical busy time periods. Danilo knew that he was serving his customers as fast as possible and that it didn't make sense to somehow pressure his customers to eat faster. Danilo's accountant observed that it appeared that customers often had to wait for their checks or for their receipts. Danilo wondered if perhaps there was another bottleneck in his restaurant.

Questions.

1. Diagram the restaurant process. Are there one or two processes in the restaurant? If there are really two processes, show the interdependencies in your diagram.

2. What could be the source of the next bottleneck now appearing in the restaurant? Describe how to use the five-step TOC process to improve (i.e., "break") this new bottleneck operation.

3. Assume that you are able to break the new bottleneck and the constraint shifts back to the line cook operation. What are some possible things Danilo could now do to elevate this constraint? Try to prioritize your ideas according to ease of implementation.

4. Assume that all the TOC-based improvements have resulted in a significant increase in the average number of customers served. However, the standard cost accounting system that Danilo's management accountant had installed when the restaurant first opened is now generating some negative efficiency variances. Specifically, it shows large increases in hours paid for expeditors and cashiers, as well as a smaller increase in hours paid for restockers. This percentage increase is larger than the percentage increase in customer volume, resulting in negative efficiency variances. Danilo is wondering whether the TOC system is creating an unanticipated problem in the process. Respond to this concern in light of the effect of TOC on traditional accounting systems.

5. The restaurant business has some unique aspects respecting personnel scheduling, specifically with respect to servers. Typically, servers make the bulk of their income based on tips. As the flow of customers declines and tables are empty, then servers have a significant decrease in their average hourly wage. Hence, Lindo's, like most restaurants, will release servers to go home as customer flow declines. Could this aspect of the restaurant industry affect the way throughput margin is measured in a throughput accounting system? Why?

NOTES

NOTES

LIST OF MODULES

MANAGEMENT ACCOUNTING—A STRATEGIC FOCUS, A MODULAR SERIES

Currently Available:

Strategy and Management Accounting (0-256-27147-X)

Management Accounting in the Age of Lean Production (0-256-27146-1)

Target Costing (0-256-27145-3)

Measuring and Managing Environmental Costs (0-256-27144-5)

Measuring and Managing Quality Costs (0-256-27143-7)

Activity-Based Management (0-256-23787-5)

Measuring and Managing Capacity (0-256-27141-0)

Measuring and Managing Indirect Costs (0-256-27140-2)

Manufacturing Overhead Allocation: Traditional and Activity Based (0-256-26392-2)

The Organizational Role of Management Accountants (0-256-26395-7)

Activity-Based Budgeting (0-256-26393-0)

The Theory of Constraints and Throughput Accounting (0-07027589-0)

Forthcoming Modules:

The Kaleidoscopic Nature of Costs: Cost Terms and Classifications

Cost Measurement Systems: Traditional and Contemporary

International Managerial Accounting

Managing Supply Chain and Make or Buy Decisions

Benchmarking for Competitor and Value Chain Analysis

Activity Based Marketing and Distribution Cost Analysis

Cost Management Using Business Process Reengineering

Cost Analysis for Pricing and Capacity Use Decisions

Cost Profit Product Mix and Volume Analysis

Product Costing in Mass Manufacturing-Process Costing

Job Costing in Mass and Lean Manufacturing Environments

Product Costing in Lean Manufacturing-Operations Costing

Joint Cost Problems in Manufacturing and Service Industries

Strategic Budgeting Part II: Multi-year Product and Profit Planning

Strategic Budgeting Part III: Long-term Capital Budgeting

Customer Profitability Analysis

Driver Based Cost Estimation Methods

Experience Based Cost Estimation Methods

Standard and Kaizen Costing

Variance Analysis

Analyzing Throughout, Mix and Yield

Inventory Management in Mass and Lean Environments

Capacity Rationing Using Linear Programming

The Historical Evolution of Cost Accounting

Absorption Cost vs. Variable Cost Systems

Management Accounting Systems and Information Technology

Measuring Preproduction Costs

PRICING AND PACKAGING

Effective immediately, all modules are priced at $4.95 list ($3.95 net). The STRATEGY AND MANAGEMENT ACCOUNTING module can be downloaded for free from our modules homepage: http//www.mhhe.com/business/accounting/modules.

Hard copies are available on request.